Six Themes
Everyone Should Know

# Psalms

Jerome F. D. Creach

Geneva
Press

*Cover designer: Rebecca Kueber*

**Library of Congress Cataloging-in-Publication Data**

Names: Creach, Jerome F. D. (Jerome Frederick Davis), 1962- author.
Title: Six themes in the Psalms everyone should know / Jerome F.D. Creach.
Description: First edition. | Louisville, Kentucky: Geneva Press, 2019. |
  Series: Six themes everyone should know series
Identifiers: LCCN 2019001550 (print) | LCCN 2019016980 (ebook) | ISBN
  9781611649604 (ebk.) | ISBN 9781571532404 (pbk. : alk. paper)
Subjects: LCSH: Bible. Psalms--Theology.
Classification: LCC BS1430.52 (ebook) | LCC BS1430.52 .C7355 2019 (print) |
  DDC 223/.206--dc23
LC record available at https://lccn.loc.gov/2019001550

# Contents

## Six Themes Everyone Should Know series

*The Bible,* by Barry Ensign-George

*Genesis,* by W. Eugene March

*Matthew,* by James E. Davison

*Luke,* by John T. Carroll

*1 and 2 Timothy,* by Thomas G. Long

*Jeremiah,* by W. Eugene March

*Exodus,* by V. Steven Parrish

*Psalms,* by Jerome F. D. Creach

# Introduction to the
## *Six Themes Everyone Should Know* series

The *Six Themes Everyone Should Know* series focuses on the study of Scripture. Bible study is vital to the lives of churches. Churches need ways of studying Scripture that can fit a variety of contexts and group needs. *Six Themes Everyone Should Know* studies offer a central feature of church adult educational programs. Their flexibility and accessibility make it possible to have short-term studies that introduce biblical books and their main themes.

*Six Themes Everyone Should Know* consists of six chapters that introduce major biblical themes. At the core of each chapter is an introduction and three major sections. These sections relate to key dimensions of Bible study. These sections ask:

- What does this biblical theme mean?
- What is the meaning of this biblical theme for the life of faith?
- What does this biblical theme mean for the church at this point in history for action?

This format presents a compact and accessible way for people in various educational settings to gain knowledge about major themes in the biblical books; to experience the impact of what Scripture means for Christian devotion to God; and to consider ways Scripture can lead to new directions for the church in action.

# Introduction to *Psalms*

At the center of the Bible is the book of Psalms, a collection of 150 prayers to be read, sung, carried in the heart, and shouted at the top of our lungs. The prayers are meant for personal and communal expression. The Psalms plumb the depths of human emotion as God's people express rage, despair, doubt, sorrow, exaltation, joy, faith, and hope. Collectively and separately, the Psalms offer a steadfast witness to God's revelation as Creator, Redeemer, and Sustainer of life. Within each psalm, as within the hearts of the worshiping community, is a deep yearning to be surrounded by God's presence, to know God's power, and to understand God's purposes.

The Hebrew title for the book of Psalms, *tehillim*, means "praise" or "songs of praise." At the heart of the Psalms is the desire to praise God for being God.

Jerome Creach has provided a means to get to the heart of the Psalms in an accessible fashion. The Psalms offer us a counter-cultural definition of happiness, not based on success or acquisition, but on the nearness of God. That God guides and protects us, as a shepherd leads and guards her sheep. The presence of God is described as a thirst-quenching wadi, a stream that appears only with the rains. When calamity strikes, we are assured that God wants and answers our prayers for help. Human beings are often the answer to prayers for help, as we have been commissioned with the awesome task of caring for all of creation. Finally, when disappointment and disillusion overwhelm all attempts at reasoned action against injustice, God stands ready to receive our angry rants. The Psalms reveal a God who desires relationship with all of creation and calls on us to reciprocate. All relationships work better with good, honest communication. The same is true for our relationship with God.

May you be blessed in your study of six themes in the book of Psalms everyone should know!

# Biblical Backgrounds to Psalms

## Author and Date

We must admit right off that precious little is known for certain about the who, when, and why of the composer of particular psalms. Psalms are notoriously difficult to date and at best can be placed in broad areas, like the monarchy or the postexilic period.

On the other hand, the psalms were in fact written by somebody in Hebrew in circumstances and for our purposes that belonged to the history of Israel. They are, in the first instance, the religious poetry of a particular community.

—James L. Mays, *Psalms*. Interpretation: A Bible Commentary for Teaching and Preaching (Louisville, KY: Westminster John Knox Press, 1994), 8.

## Major Concerns

Psalms were written for the annual national festivals and their celebration of the Lord's providence in the world and Israel's destiny. The psalms would be used for processions, entrance ceremonies, pilgrimage songs, and liturgical agenda as well as for general praise. They were also used in times of disaster and danger that affected the entire community and brought it together for lament and appeal to God for help. . . . The place of the Davidic king in Israel's life and the rituals that interpreted and celebrated his importance were another generative source of psalm composition.

—Mays, *Psalms*, 10.

## Importance

. . . the Psalter can be read as a Davidic, messianic book of prayer and praise. In it we hear the messiah speak about the kingdom of God and pray for the vindication of the reign of God in the messiah's salvation. By the existence of the book as Scripture and liturgy we are invited to enter into and join in this messianic prayer and praise. We are given a way to find our place in the coming reign of God.

—Mays, *Psalms*, 18.

*Although "happy" may not be the best translation of the Hebrew word ("blessed" may be better), it is useful in engaging us in conversation about what we seek after and what we think brings contentment.*

## Chapter 1

# The Meaning of Happiness

**Psalms 1 and 2** These psalms describe "happy" people as those who know the joy of being rooted in and dependent on God.

## Prayer
O God, teach us the way to true happiness. Lead us to the waters that satisfy, to those that flow from your presence. Plant us near you that you may nurture us and teach us your way, for we know that your way is the way to life. Lead us away from actions, activities, and words that are deceitful and destructive. Set us on the path Jesus walks, for we know that he will lead us to a life that is abundant and full. In the name of Jesus, who followed you perfectly, we pray. Amen.

## Introduction
What does it mean to be happy? "Happy" is the first word in the Psalter, and there are reasons to think it is a central theme in the book. The word "happy" also begins the last line of Psalm 2. Psalms 1 and 2 together form the introduction to the Psalter. The word also appears in other prominent places in the Psalms. The book of Psalms has five divisions or "books" (Psalms 1–41; 42–72; 73–89; 90–106; 107–150). "Happy" introduces Psalm 41, the last psalm in book 1 of the Psalter. So it seems that those who wrote the Psalms and preserved them had this subject in mind.

The Psalms, however, offer a perspective on happiness that is quite different from the common conception of happiness in our culture. The Hebrew word that the NRSV translates as "happy" (*ashre*, pronounced ash-ray) is difficult to capture in English, so this translation is not altogether adequate. Our culture tends to associate happiness with enjoyment, pleasure, and self-satisfaction. Psalm 1 insists that happiness comes from being rooted in God and delighting in God's teachings. As Psalm 1 and other psalms make clear, this often means a "happy" person faces hardship and suffering.

Happiness according to the Psalms is a state of being that results from being close to God and obedient to God's will.[1] Jesus uses the equivalent Greek term to introduce the Beatitudes. Many translations use the term "blessed," which may be a better translation in Psalm 1 (cf. Matthew 5:1). It refers to the kind of life, behavior, and mind-set that creates a deep and abiding contentment. It is the kind of life God endorses. It speaks of a life that leads to joy, but not necessarily to ease and abundance. The book of Psalms will give insight into that kind of life.

## A Basic Theme: Happiness as Dependence on God

The Psalms never define happiness. Mainly they describe certain kinds of people as happy, as in Psalm 1:1, "Happy are those . . ." In Psalm 1 and elsewhere "happy" describes a group of people called "the righteous." The word "righteous" is a common word in the Psalms (it appears fifty-two times in the book). It is the Psalms' favorite designation for those who live according to God's intentions, that is, for those who are truly "happy." Nevertheless, many contemporary Christians may be uncomfortable with this language. There is a common assumption that the word "righteous" derives from narrow judgmental attitudes of the sort the Pharisees displayed (Matthew 23:13–28). So, as Psalm 1 introduces the model person of faith as righteous, some readers may be inclined to ignore the message for fear that it encourages self-congratulation and self-righteousness. To associate righteousness with self-righteousness, however, is to misunderstand the word and what the Psalms are saying about happiness. Two features of

1. J. Clinton McCann Jr. "The Book of Psalms" in *The New Interpreter's Bible*, vol. 4 ed. Leander E. Keck (Nashville: Abingdon Press, 1996), 686.

he word "righteous" help clarify its meaning and, in turn, clarify what it means to be happy.

*The speaker in the Psalms (the psalmist) never uses the word "righteous" when speaking of himself or herself.* It is always a third-person reference. It is, essentially, a divine evaluation of a person or group of people. The term is never a claim of moral superiority. In fact, one of the key characteristics of the righteous is their humility. They do not think too highly of themselves.

*The Psalms speak of the righteous in relation to the "wicked."* The wicked represent the opposite of what God desires and therefore psalms often describe the righteous as not being like them. The wicked are self-centered, greedy, and full of pride in themselves (Psalm 5:4–5). They believe they created themselves and can rely on themselves; therefore, they believe God has no control over and no concern about what they do (Psalm 64:1–6).

Psalm 10 gives an extended portrait of the wicked that lays out these characteristics:

For the wicked boast of the desires of their heart,
    those greedy for gain curse and renounce the LORD.
In the pride of their countenance the wicked say, "God will
      not seek it out";
    all their thoughts are, "There is no God." (Psalm 10:3–4)

The psalm goes on to say that the wicked, with their heightened sense of autonomy, take advantage of others. The ones they take advantage of are called "righteous." For this reason the psalmist calls the righteous "afflicted" and "poor." They are vulnerable to the attacks of the wicked.

What makes the righteous stand out most is that they call on the Lord for help in their trouble. In Psalm 64 the psalmist prays, "Hide me from the secret plots of the wicked" (v. 2). Then the psalm ends by urging the righteous to depend on God for protection: "Let the righteous rejoice in the LORD and take refuge in him. Let all the upright in heart glory" (v. 10). As Psalm 37:39 says, God "is their refuge in the time of trouble." Psalm 1 suggests the righteous need protection, and it insists that the way of the wicked may be prosperous in the short run but leads to destruction (Psalm 1:4–6).

This set of connections suggests, therefore, that to be happy is to be humble, vulnerable, and dependent on God. Happiness in this sense is very different from the shallow, materialistic understanding of happiness our culture promotes.

### The Life of Faith: Meditating on the Law as a Way to Happiness

What makes a person happy? The question is the subject of much debate and study today. Some universities offer courses on happiness. There is even a scholarly journal devoted to exploring the question of what makes us happy and how we experience happiness.[2]

Most conceptions of happiness in our culture are tied to what a person owns or does. In the Psalms, however, happiness is determined by the degree to which a person relies on God to shape his or her life. Psalm 1 declares that the primary instrument of that divine shaping is "the law of the LORD" (v. 2).

"Law" here translates the Hebrew word *torah* which has the general meaning "instruction." The word in the Old Testament may refer to guidelines for life as broad-ranging as prophetic oracles (Isaiah 1:10) and Moses' speeches in Deuteronomy (Deuteronomy 31:24). It does not refer to a burdensome legal code that restricts life. Torah includes laws like those in the law codes of Exodus, Leviticus, and Deuteronomy. Those laws are torah because they instruct and illuminate a way of life consistent with the will of God.[3] Thus, Psalm 1 says that the righteous find life's fulfillment in torah because torah points to the Lord's purpose for the world.

With this understanding of law, it makes sense that those who are "happy" "meditate day and night" on it. The word translated "meditate" often means "to mumble" or "speak under the breath" (Joshua 1:8). Those who meditate on torah, verse 3 says, are "like trees planted by streams of water." The image of the tree appears numerous times in the Old Testament, and it occurs with nearly exact language in Jeremiah 17:8: "They shall be like a tree planted by water." Yet Psalm 1:3 is unique in that it includes the term

2. *Journal of Happiness Studies: An Interdisciplinary Forum on Subjective Well-Being.* ISSN: 1389–4978 (Print), 1573–7780 (Online).
3. James Luther Mays, *Psalms,* Interpretation: A Bible Commentary for Teaching and Preaching (Louisville, KY: Westminster John Knox Press, 1994), 43.

"streams" (*pelagim*), which has a somewhat specialized meaning in the Old Testament. In most passages it refers to the water channels on the holy mountain where the temple is located (Psalms 46:4; 65:9). Ancient Israelites thought of the temple as a paradise, a place that produced abundant life because of God's presence. We see this in Ezekiel's vision of trees planted by the stream that flows from the temple (Ezekiel 47:12).

Psalms 52:10 and 92:13–15 both speak of those who follow God's way ("the righteous") as trees planted in the temple. Psalm 1:3 speaks of them with similar language; it is distinctive in that it says they are secure because they meditate on torah. This seems to mean that torah has the same life-giving potential as the temple and gives access to God's presence just as the temple did. Since Psalm 1 presents torah as instruction that presumably includes the Psalms, it seems likely that the first psalm invites readers to find a secure place near God by reading and meditating on this book. Thus, Psalm 1 introduces the Psalms (and the rest of Scripture) as a kind of spiritual temple in which the reader becomes planted near the divine presence. A person becomes "happy" by following the guidance of God's instruction.

## The Church: Proclaim Jesus Christ, the Happy Man

The church has a significant challenge to define happiness as the Psalms do since so many definitions of happiness in our culture are based on materialism and consumerism. Perhaps the best resource to do that is the church's traditional understanding of Jesus Christ as the quintessential "happy" person. The first words of Psalm 1 reads, "Happy is the man" in some translations. Though many translators take the opening line to refer to all persons who seek the way of the Lord (and thus translate "those who"), "the man" has suggested to many the model person, Jesus Christ.

The Orthodox Church places special emphasis on this identification of Jesus as the "happy" one. In worship a priest turns to an icon of Jesus and recites the words of the psalm as a way of recognizing that he lived the life Psalm 1 describes in a way no one else ever has. This one who perfectly walked in the way of righteousness thus embodies the path described in the first psalm. As the church proclaims Christ, it necessarily declares what true happiness is and with that, the true meaning of righteousness.

The church today has a unique opportunity to inculcate this perspective on happiness. As the example of the Orthodox tradition illustrates, the church may proclaim the meaning of happiness in relation to Jesus Christ as part of its proclamation of the gospel. Just as important, however, it can model this happiness as it works to fulfill its mission to the poor and suffering people of the world.

When the church ministers to those who are suffering, it does so not out of a sense that those who minister have something the poor need. Rather, they recognize they have a need for partnership with the poor because Scripture recognizes the poor as "blessed" or "happy" (Luke 6:20; Matthew 5:3). In a culture in which "winning" is rewarded at all costs and "winners" are heralded as supreme models of success, the church must declare once again that Christ-likeness is the only way to true happiness.

The late Fred Rogers, a man who had a deep understanding of the church's mission, met a boy who had cerebral palsy. Mr. Rogers asked the boy to pray for him. The boy was thrilled and encouraged to look on the bright side of life in a way he had never been able to do. Later a journalist, who was authoring a story on Rogers's work with children, complimented him on the way he boosted the boy's self-esteem. Mr. Rogers didn't see the encounter the same way. He told the journalist that he really did cherish the boy's prayers, for, he said, "I think that anyone who has gone through challenges like that must be very close to God."[4] Mr. Rogers was saying essentially that the boy, because he had endured incredible hardships, was in fact "happy." His greatest challenge was to recognize his favored status before God and live into the happiness of that relationship.

## For Reflection and Action

1. Make a list of three things that you associate with the word "happy." Then write a prayer based on Psalm 1 that asks God for true happiness. How many of the items on the list can you include in your prayer? How much of what you relate to happiness is related to your relationship with God?

4. Tom Junod, "Can You Say . . . Hero?" *Esquire* (November 1998).

2. Who would you call "happy" as Psalm 1 speaks of happiness, and why would you apply that label to him or her?

3. What would "meditating" on God's word look like for you? What can you do to keep the words and truth of Scripture always in your mind and heart?

4. What do you think of the claim that Jesus is the quintessential happy man, using the description of "happy" in this chapter?

One of the key lines is verse 1b: *"I shall not want."* It challenges our natural inclinations to desire and seek after so many things, and it draws our attention to God's provision of what matters most.

## Chapter 2

# The Lord Is My Shepherd

**Psalm 23** One of the best-known passages in the Bible, this psalm evokes trust and faith through the image of God as shepherd, the one who guides us to all good things.

## Prayer

Eternal God, you led your people Israel through the wilderness, and you carried them like little lambs when they were far from home. We know that you have carried us also. From birth you have watched over us and nurtured us with your love. May we now submit to your shepherding care that you may lead us to the waters that satisfy and to pastures where you feed us. Remind us that as you direct our paths toward righteousness, you prepare us for the dark valleys we inevitably travel, and that in them we are never alone. In the name of Jesus our shepherd, we pray. Amen.

## Introduction

Psalm 23 is one of the best-known passages in the Bible. It is a staple of funeral liturgies in all Christian denominations. The psalm is frequently set to music. It is perhaps the only passage of Scripture recognized by its chapter reference. When someone says "the Twenty-third," we know what that means.

The enduring popularity of the psalm is due to the beauty of the image that opens the psalm: "The LORD is my shepherd." This figure of speech in turn guides the entire poem. For that reason, this chapter will explore the meaning of the shepherd image more than anything else.

"Shepherd" is a metaphor in Psalm 23. A metaphor is a powerful figure of speech, like a simile in that it defines one thing by reference to another. A simile makes direct comparison with words such as "as" or "like" (e.g., Psalm 42:1, "As a deer longs for flowing streams, so my soul longs for you, O God"). A metaphor, however, is stronger than a simile. It does not merely compare two things. It equates them. Psalm 23 does not say, "The LORD is *like* a shepherd to me" but "The LORD *is* my shepherd" (v. 1a). The metaphor essentially says, "All that a shepherd is and does, that's who and what God is to me."

Although the shepherd metaphor dominates the psalm, another image appears in verse 5, namely, God as host. This image comes from the ancient practice of hospitality. Travelers in the ancient world faced threats from the elements, from wild animals, and from criminals (see Luke 10:25–37). The threats increased at night since there were usually no hotels or inns for lodging. Therefore, travelers relied on the hospitality of strangers who offered refreshment, food, and safety. In Psalm 23 the image of God as host fits neatly within the larger metaphor of God as shepherd. Both ways of thinking about God focus on God's protection and guiding care. The place of safety and nourishment is the "house of the LORD" (v. 6).

## A Basic Theme: The Lord Is My Shepherd

The statement "The LORD is my shepherd" has several dimensions of meaning. This figure of speech draws from experiences of those who tend sheep. This was a common activity and vocation for people in the ancient Near East. Visitors to the region today may still observe shepherds at work. Shepherds guide their sheep to food and water. They lead them from danger. In the ancient world, shepherds hired to care for the sheep of others were accountable for the welfare of the flock. If a predator took one of the sheep, the shepherd had to prove that he or she tried to protect the sheep (Amos 3:12). For those who tended their own flock there was a built-in financial incentive to guard against threats to the safety of the sheep. Some Israelites also grew emotionally attached to their sheep like we might be attached to pets (see 2 Samuel 12:1–6).

This background helps us understand a basic aspect of the metaphor: God cares for the psalmist as a shepherd cares for sheep. Just as sheep depend on the shepherd to find food and water and to live free of life-threatening circumstances, so the psalmist relies on the Lord. As James Luther Mays says, however, "the notion of being shepherd of persons opens up a background of tradition that is far broader than animal husbandry."[1] Many leaders presented themselves as shepherds of people. They wanted their subjects to see them as benevolent, caring rulers. We see this in the Old Testament's introduction of David in 1 Samuel 16. The Lord directed Samuel to anoint one of Jesse's sons to be king of Israel. The one God had chosen, however, was not there because he was tending the sheep (1 Samuel 16:11). Later, when David volunteered to fight Goliath, he declared he was ready for the task because he had defended his father's sheep against lions and bears (1 Samuel 17:31–37). The people expected their leaders to care for them exactly this way. They knew some shepherds were careless or even fed off the flock (Ezekiel 34:1–10). But a faithful shepherd like David risked his life for the sheep (John 10:11). Psalm 23 assumes God is this kind of shepherd for those who rely on God's protection.

Most of the Old Testament's descriptions of God as shepherd pertain to God's leading the people of Israel. God led them like a shepherd through the wilderness on their way to the promised land (Psalms 77:20; 80:1). When they went into exile in Babylon there was a promise that he would lead them home as a shepherd seeks out lost sheep (Isaiah 40:11). Psalm 23 contains echoes of the wilderness experience: verse 23:1b recalls Deuteronomy 2:7 in declaring the Israelites "lacked nothing" in the wilderness; "He leads me in right paths" (v. 3) is similar to Exodus 15:13; "You prepare a table before me" (v. 5) sounds like Psalm 78:19 that speaks of God spreading a table in the wilderness. Hence, Psalm 23 declares that God leads the psalmist as God has led the people of Israel.

## The Life of Faith: God as Shepherd in a Consumer Culture

One of the most remarkable claims of Psalm 23 comes in the statement that follows the opening metaphor: "I shall not want" (v. 1b). The Lord's guiding presence is all that the psalmist needs.

1. *Psalms,* Interpretation: A Bible Commentary for Teaching and Preaching (Louisville, KY: Westminster John Knox Press, 1994), 117.

This claim is especially important when heard in our consumer culture. The statement is open to two kinds of misinterpretations:

*Misinterpretation 1. A relationship with the divine shepherd causes us to reorganize our priorities and want little.* The idea is that we change our thinking about what we need and determine that most material goods are not necessary, which suggests that we should live a life of self-denial and austerity. This misunderstanding points toward asceticism, a commitment to denying oneself pleasure. Ascetics have always had a significant role in the church as they commit themselves to prayer and service while eschewing the pleasures of the world. The problem with reading Psalm 23:1b as a nod toward asceticism, however, is that it does not account for the images of abundance that fill the psalm. The psalmist speaks of God's leading to food and water (v. 2) and to hosting an abundant feast (v. 5). Indeed, there is nothing in Psalm 23 that suggests a reader would be led to consider what to go without.

*Misinterpretation 2. God gives us all the material riches we want.* We may observe the second type of misunderstanding in the so-called health-and-wealth gospel. It is an audacious claim that God wants us to be rich in material things and so gives us all our hearts desire. This view reduces the language of abundance to references to mundane and base desires, which makes little sense in the context of the Psalter and the Bible as a whole. This runs counter to the rest of the Psalter where those who depend on God profess to being "poor" and "needy" while those the psalms call "wicked" enjoy material abundance (see Psalm 73:12).

So what does the psalmist mean by "I shall not want?" The answer seems to lie in the psalmist's recognition that God's presence is the most valuable blessing any person can have. It does not deny the need and desire for food, safety, and material goods, but they all take second place to God's presence. Psalm 27 may help us understand this overwhelming desire for God. There the psalmist says, "One thing I asked of the LORD, that will I seek after: to live in the house of the LORD all the days of my life, to behold the beauty of the LORD, and to inquire in his temple" (Psalm 27:4). This psalm contains a remarkable statement, namely, that the psalmist seeks after only "one thing," and that is to be near God's presence. Psalm 23:1b likewise recognizes that fellowship with God is what makes life rich. It does not deny the need for other things, but it suggests that the "things of this world" are stale and tasteless compared to the fellowship with God.

## The Church: Proclaiming the Promises of God as Shepherd
The image of God as shepherd has potential to shape profoundly the church's understanding of God and God's work in our lives. Congregations might well choose to present God's nature and deeds primarily with this image, and they would have strong scriptural support. As noted above, the image of God as shepherd is a dominant understanding of how God led Israel (Isaiah 40:11), and it is also a prominent image of Jesus in the New Testament (John 10). Churches with stained-glass windows may have one that represents Jesus as a shepherd. A popular Tiffany window, sometimes called the Twenty-third Psalm window, depicts Jesus with sheep following closely on each side while he carries a lamb in his arms. Such a window provides a profound visual proclamation of the nature of God in Jesus Christ. Congregations without such windows might acquire a piece of artwork that shows this type of scene and place it in a prominent location. It is appropriate for the church to highlight this intimate portrait of a savior who protects and guides us through life. The picture essentially refutes the idea of a clock-maker God who is removed from the daily challenges of believers.

What exactly is the church's message concerning the Divine Shepherd, and how should it be communicated? One message the church has often embraced comes from Psalm 23:4: "Even though I walk through the darkest valley, I fear no evil; for you are with me; your rod and your staff—they comfort me." The more traditional translation of the place reference is more wooden: "the valley of the shadow of death." For generations it has suggested God's guidance from this life to the next. The end of Psalm 23 announces the ultimate hope in the life to come: "I shall dwell in the house of the LORD" (v. 6b). Thus, Psalm 23, along with images of Jesus the shepherd, has been a popular resource for funerals and memorial services. This continues to be a proper use of the psalm and the image of God as shepherd.

Even more important, however, is the potential for the shepherd image to call believers to faithfulness in the present life. To have God as shepherd means that God directs every aspect of life. Far from being removed from our circumstances, Psalm 23 declares that the Divine Shepherd is near to us in even the darkest valleys. Most significantly, "shepherd" implies authority. In the ancient world the shepherd image was popular with kings because people understood how the relationship between shepherd and sheep worked: sheep were incredibly vulnerable, nearly helpless on their own; they needed the shepherd to protect them, lead them to food and water, and guide them from danger. For the relationship to work, however, sheep must follow the shepherd. In a culture that values rugged individualism, the notion of God as shepherd is a primary conception that calls people to depend on God.

## For Reflection and Action

1. In Psalm 23 the psalmist declares that because of God's shepherding care, "goodness and mercy" pursue him or her. Write a few sentences about a time in your life when you felt this was true for you. What made you feel that goodness and mercy were with you?

2. Psalm 23 expands the image of God as shepherd by also including the image of God as host. How does God "host" us? What kind of protection and comfort does God give?

3. What does it mean to you that God leads you into "right paths?" How does God provide such leadership for you?

4. The ultimate destination for the psalmist is the "house of the LORD," which seems to refer to the place of worship. In what ways have you found safety and guidance in a worshiping community?

*The psalmist is far from home and far from the place of worship that gives proper orientation to goodness and truth. Explore how the worshiping community serves as "home" for many people.*

## Chapter 3

# Thirsting for God

**Psalms 42–43** These two psalms describe the psalmist's "thirst" for God, which is found in the worshiping community.

**Psalm 63** This psalm also begins with the metaphor of thirst to describe a desire for God, especially as the psalmist seeks safety from enemies.

## Prayer

Creator and Redeemer God, you alone can truly satisfy us. You made us in your love to have fellowship with you. When we rebelled against you, you sought us out and drew us back to yourself. Your steadfast love is better than life itself. Yet we often seek our identity and our fulfillment in short-term pleasures our culture urges us to thirst after. Teach us again that we find our purpose only when we find ourselves in you. Remind us—we who want so much—that when we have you, we have everything we need. Amen.

## Introduction

Saint Augustine opens his *Confessions of a Sinner* by saying that human beings cannot be content unless they are in close relationship with their Maker: "The thought of you stirs him so deeply that he cannot be content unless he praises you, because you made us for yourself and our hearts find no peace until they rest in you."[1]

1. Saint Augustine, *Confessions of a Sinner,* trans. R. S. Pine-Coffin (New York: Penguin Books, 1961), 1.

The book of Psalms expresses this need and longing for God more than any other book in the Bible. The psalms speak of the desire for God as "thirst." They say essentially that we need the Creator as much as the body needs water.

This chapter includes Psalms 42, 43, and 63. Psalms 42 and 43, however, are really a single psalm. Our English Bibles separate them because they appear as two psalms in Hebrew. They have two common lines that hold them together: (1) They share the refrain "Why are you cast down, O my soul, and why are you disquieted within me? Hope in God; for I shall again praise him, my help and my God" (Psalms 42:5, 11; 43:5). (2) They also have in common the lament about an enemy: "Why must I walk about mournfully because the enemy oppresses me?" (42:9; 43:2).

Psalm 63 begins with the metaphor of thirst to speak of the desire for God's presence, especially as the psalmist seeks protection from enemies. This psalm, like Psalms 42–43, understands that God's life-giving presence is found in the temple. Psalms 42–43 speak of the temple experience in terms of the joy of being part of the worshiping community. The shared experience with "the living God" (v. 2) gives perspective on life that those outside the community do not have. Thus, those who do not understand the God the psalmist worships taunt, "'Where is your God?'" (Psalm 42:3, 10). In Psalm 63 the enemies threaten the psalmist's life, so the psalm focuses on God's protection found in the holy place.

## A Basic Theme: Thirsting for the Presence of God

Psalm 42 opens with a verbal image of desire for God that is unique in the Psalter: "As a deer longs for flowing streams, so my soul longs for you, O God. My soul thirsts for God, for the living God" (vv. 1–2). The expression translated "flowing streams" refers to streambeds called wadis. When rains came, they filled with water and temporarily became streams, but most of the time they were dry gullies (see 1 Kings 17:1–7). The psalmist is like a deer that brays desperately when he comes to a wadi that is dry. That longing for water is an emblem of the psalmist's longing to be in God's presence in the temple.

The psalmist's desire to be in God's presence is the main subject of Psalms 42–43, and this theme dominates the movement of the poem. The initial declarations about thirsting for God (42:1–2) give way to a question that represents the main problem: "When shall I come and behold the face of God?" (42:2). The taunt of the enemy ("'Where is your God?'") stings because the psalmist is far from the holy place, and so God seems absent (42:3). Memories of being among worshipers in the temple fuel the pain (42:4). The psalmist remembers being there for one of Israel's festivals, but now he or she is far away. Geographical references in 42:6 seem to locate the psalmist far in the north, on Mt. Hermon where the waters of the Jordan begin. In Psalm 42:7 the image of water returns, but with a different connotation. In Psalm 42:1–2 water represented life, with God as the source, but in Psalm 42:7 water becomes threatening, a symbol of trouble and despair. Being inundated is a common image for life-threatening trouble in the Psalms (69:1). In Psalm 42 these threatening waters represent the psalmist's distress over God's absence. They are waters of God, not chaos ("your cataracts"; "your waves and your billows"), because the psalmist experiences what seems like God's punishment. The psalm turns to God's command of steadfast love (v. 8), which removes the threat just described.

These two psalms respond to the enemy's taunt and the recurring doubt and turmoil it creates with hope to finally arrive at "the altar of God" (43:4). With that as the goal, the psalmist is able to answer her own doubts with "hope in God" (42:11; 43:5), hope based on the anticipation of being in the presence of God and with worshipers who gather to praise.

Psalm 63 opens with the image of thirst that is almost identical to Psalm 42:2: "my soul thirsts for you" (v. 1a). It continues the metaphor with the image of being in the wilderness: "my flesh faints for you, as in a dry and weary land where there is no water" (v. 1b). As in Psalms 42–43, the psalmist in Psalm 63 is at a distance from God's temple. That distance creates the "thirst" for God's presence.

## The Life of Faith: The Living God as the One Who Satisfies Thirst

For what do we thirst? What do we need to make life rich and good more than anything else? We are constantly bombarded with advertising that suggests we need all sorts of things (and experiences), most of them being products the advertisers are selling:

a new car, a certain food or drink, a line of clothing that gives a particular "look." It is easy to believe such messages because the commercials present images of success and satisfaction that seem compelling. The problem, however, is that these material things do not satisfy our thirst for satisfaction at a deeper level. They merely give the illusion of success and contentment.

The psalmist thirsts for "the living God" (Psalm 42:2). The phrase does not emphasize merely that God is alive and not dead. The expression in Psalm 42:2 suggests rather that God oversees life itself and is in charge of life, with power to give it or take it away. This is clearly the meaning in Isaiah's prophecy against King Sennacherib of Assyria (see 2 Kings 19 and Isaiah 37). Sennacherib surrounded Jerusalem and had his messenger order the city to surrender. In distress, King Hezekiah sent word to Isaiah that the Assyrian king had come to "mock the living God" (2 Kings 19:4, 16; Isaiah 37:4, 17). In the prophecy that followed, Isaiah declared that Sennacherib was a fool because he believed he controlled the movement of history. That power belonged only to the God of Israel, the "living God." Put in a positive way, "the living God" is the fountain and source of life. Therefore, the psalmist desires more than anything else to be in God's presence.

The psalmist's thirst for the living God reflects a struggle with the prevailing culture. In the world of the psalmist there were many deities some believed powerful enough to create and enhance life. This was true of the Canaanite god Baal, whose followers believed caused the earth to give its produce. Such gods were attractive because they existed solely to give humans the material goods that sustained life and enriched the pocketbook. The Israelites declared that the "living God" had that power, but their God did not simply make them richer in money and crops. Indeed, the living God entered into relationship with them, laid claim to their lives, and directed their lives toward goodness. Whereas the main reward for worshiping Baal was to receive a rich harvest, the greatest reward for worshiping the living God of Israel was to "look upon" God, to be in God's presence (Psalm 63:2). The greatest gift the living God gave was not crops but steadfast love. The psalmist knew that in relationship with God one found life. So the psalmist declared, "Your steadfast love is better than life" (Psalm 63:3). The psalm bids us seek that same source of life, the one who is "better than life."

## The Church: Satisfying Thirst in the Gathering of Believers

The church has a unique opportunity to invite worshipers into an experience with the "living God" each week as the congregation gathers for worship. The question is, how should the church present, plan, and carry out worship that allows this kind of encounter? If we follow the hints in the psalms, at least three elements are crucial.

*Worship should give voice to the truth that the gospel is countercultural.* We claim that we find power in weakness because God brings salvation to the world through the death of Jesus. Such ideas may seem like nonsense to those outside the church. They may question the truth of it just as they questioned the psalmist ("'Where is your God?'"; Psalm 42:3, 10). Therefore, it is important to articulate that what gives life is "not of this world" and those who embrace it are "resident aliens."[2]

*Part of the church's invitation to meet the living God should be an invitation to experience beauty.* Although the spoken word is important, the church should also present sights, sounds, and perhaps even smells that please the senses and that communicate God's majesty. Many Protestant Christians overlook beauty, but their faith is diminished when they do. Psalm 27:4 speaks of a desire "to behold the beauty of the LORD." Psalm 63:2 speaks of this as well: "So I have looked upon you in the sanctuary, beholding your power and glory" (see Psalm 42:2). Although the Old Testament says emphatically that no one can see God (Exodus 33:20), there are signs of God's presence humans can experience with all the senses. Solomon built the temple to look like paradise (1 Kings 6:29–36), and he overlaid it with gold (1 Kings 6:22). Few churches have a budget that would allow an imitation! Nevertheless, the thoughtful use of vestments, banners, and seasonal decorations, as well as the beauty of music is appropriate to complement the spoken word. They can all point to God's presence and can add to the sense that the living God meets the worshiper in the sanctuary.

---

2. See Stanley Hauerwas and William Willimon, *Resident Aliens: Life in the Christian Colony* (Nashville: Abingdon Press, 1989).

*Fellowship should go with worship.* Much of what the psalmist describes as life-giving is belonging to a community of people who share a commitment to God's work. There must be time and space for worshipers to share their lives and experiences with one another, care for one another, and strengthen bonds of friendship. Many churches do this regularly by having a coffee hour before or after the worship service. It would be easy to dismiss this as nothing more than a snack. It should be conceived and presented, however, as an extension of what happens at the Communion table. The connections that happen in that setting should make the worshiper feel with the psalmist that "my soul is satisfied as with a rich feast" (Psalm 63:5).

## For Reflection and Action

1. The next time you are in a worship service watch how people find fellowship with God and one another. Does it occur during the singing of hymns, in the sacraments, through hearing the Word read and proclaimed? Share with others how you perceive people satisfying a "thirst."

2. How does the "living God" of Psalm 42 differ from popular ideas about God in our culture?

3. Have you ever felt that no one around you understood what your faith gives you? What is that experience like?

4. In what ways does the church supply protection, shelter, and safety for you? For others in our society?

*esus quoted from Psalm 22, and the Gospel writers
used it to frame the passion not because Psalm 22
predicted Jesus' suffering but because Jesus' suffering
followed a typical pattern of the righteous sufferer in
the Old Testament.*

## Chapter 4

# Praying to God for Help

**Psalm 22**   One of the best examples of a prayer for help by an
individual in the Psalms, it had a profound bearing on the Gospel
accounts of Jesus' passion.

## Prayer
O God, in Jesus Christ you have come and stood with us in the
depths of pain and suffering. So we dare to cry out to you with
petitions for justice and cries for comfort, believing that you hear
and answer us; that you attend the needs of those who are hungry,
those who live with the threat of disease for themselves and for
their children, the victims of discrimination and prejudice, and
those who have suffered from floods, earthquakes, and other natural disasters. Attend our needs, O God, and make us instruments of
your peace and healing. In the name of Jesus, we pray. Amen.

## Introduction
One of the most basic impulses in religious faith is to plead to God
for help when we suffer. But what form should our prayers for help
take? How should we talk with God about our suffering? Most
Christians learn to pray with the Lord's Prayer (Matt. 6:9–13), but
it does not include any direct complaint about suffering or petition for deliverance from it. While the New Testament is short on
prayers for this purpose, the Psalms are filled with them! In this

chapter we explore a type of psalm often called a prayer for help by an individual (there are also community versions like Psalms 44 and 74). Some prefer to call these prayers "laments." The lament or complaint is only one element of these psalms, but they stand out as a part of prayer that is underdeveloped in most Christian circles.

Psalm 22 is a robust example of the individual prayers for help. These prayers typically include:

1. a direct address to God;
2. description of trouble that often has a complaint or protest;
3. a plea for God to act, to come and help;
4. a profession of trust and confidence that God will hear and act; and
5. a promise to praise God and to make vows or offer sacrifices in response to God's actions.

Psalm 22 had a profound influence on the New Testament. According to Matthew 27:46 and Mark 15:34, Jesus quoted verse 1 during his suffering on the cross. Much of the rest of the psalm served as a template for the Gospel writers as they composed the story of the crucifixion. So while the New Testament does not present prayers of this type explicitly as examples for how we should pray, the Gospels offer Psalm 22 implicitly as a model of how Jesus himself prayed. Through this psalm Jesus "gives all of his followers who are afflicted permission and encouragement to pray for help. He shows that faith includes holding the worst of life up to God."[1]

## A Basic Theme: Complaining to God about Suffering

Psalm 22 models a way of praying that is brutally honest and rooted deeply in trust in God. Verses 1–21a address God, describe the psalmist's trouble, and offer a plea for God to act. Verse 1a contains one of the boldest complaints in Scripture: "My God, my God, why have you forsaken me?" If the prayer encourages us to hold up the worst of life to God, this line encourages us to be brutally honest with God about our distress, even if it means accusing God of unfaithfulness. As verses 1b–2 show, the problem is that God has not answered the psalmist's prayer for relief from suffering ("Why

1. James L. Mays, *Psalms*, Interpretation: A Bible Commentary for Teaching and Preaching (Louisville, KY: Westminster John Knox Press, 1994), 106.

are you so far from . . . my groaning?"). In verses 3–5, however, the psalmist quickly puts this complaint in the context of faith. Although God seems far away, this is the same God who was with the ancestors. They cried to and trusted God and "were not put to shame" (v. 5).

The psalmist describes the situation of trouble in more detail in verses 6–8; enemies ridicule and taunt the psalmist because of that trouble. In verses 9–11 the psalmist again remembers God's salvation in the past. Even from birth the psalmist looked to God for protection. That declaration, in turn, leads to the psalmist's first petition: "Do not be far from me" (v. 11).

The psalmist describes the trouble again and more extensively in verses 12–18. Once again the nature of the trouble is not clear, but the psalmist speaks of being near death (vv. 14–15). The enemies surround the psalmist like ravenous beasts. They are like "strong bulls of Bashan" (v. 12); they open their mouths like lions (v. 13; see v. 21); they are "dogs" that encircle. In ancient Israel wild dogs wandered in packs and presented a threat to those who were weak and alone. The psalmist feels like this in the face of the enemies. As verses 17–18 make clear, however, the animals are metaphors for enemies who are awaiting the psalmist's demise. They can't wait to enrich themselves with what the psalmist leaves behind. The petition in verse 19 again focuses on God's being near: "Do not be far away!" The psalmist calls God "my help" and pleads, "Come quickly to my aid."

The power of the prayer and the potential for it to serve as a model for us rest both in the extreme, unrestrained language of complaint and the sure faith with which the psalmist prays. The opening question ("My God, my God, why have you forsaken me?") lets us know there is no restriction on what we can say to God. We can lay our souls bare before God. The psalm suggests that God is not offended and perhaps even welcomes such bold prayer. It is only possible to pray so boldly, however, when we also recall God's saving work in the past. The psalmist prays as one of God's people and, as such, as one who remembers God's faithfulness that elicited Israel's praise in ages past (v. 3).

## The Life of Faith: Out of Trouble Comes Praise
The psalmist complains to God with full awareness that God has been faithful in the past, and the psalmist expects God to act

again in the current situation. But readers may be surprised when verses 21b–31 shift from complaint to praise and thanksgiving. In fact, this is typical of prayers for help in the Psalter. There is some debate about what caused this radical shift in these prayers. Some students of the Bible propose that the statement of praise and thanksgiving came after a priest or prophet gave an oracle assuring the person that God would deliver.[2] That seems a logical explanation for how these prayers developed. As they now appear in the Psalter, however, as in Psalm 22, the two parts of the psalm are inextricably bound to each other. The result is that complaint and petition are grounded in trust.

In verse 21b the psalmist reports confidently that God has acted. So the psalmist enters the sanctuary to worship, to give thanks for the renewed state God has granted. It is important to notice that the psalmist's thanksgiving is not a private affair. The one who gives thanks does so in the midst of a congregation and tells of God's name to "my brothers and sisters" (v. 22). The psalmist calls them to praise. "You who fear the LORD" (v. 23) and "the poor" (v. 26) identify God's people as those who stand humbly before God. "Poor" here translates the Hebrew word *anawim*. The word does not refer to an economic condition but to a condition of the heart. The poor are those who seek the Lord with their whole hearts (see the expression "those who seek" God in v. 26b). Thus, the psalmist identifies with people who recognize they depend on God. Out of this sense of dependence and vulnerability comes praise and thanksgiving for God, who has mercy on such people (v. 24).

In verses 27–31 the congregation broadens as the psalmist gives an amazingly inclusive vision of worshipers. "All the ends of the earth" refers to the outermost limits of the habitable world, the farthest reaches of God's creation (v. 27). Geographically, there is no limit to who makes up the congregation. "All the families of the nations" shows that there is no ethnic or tribal identity that places a person outside the bounds of the worshiping community. But the psalmist does not stop there. "All who sleep in the earth bow down" (v. 29). It is not certain if this means those who have died or those, like the psalmist, who are in the throes of death.

2. J. Clinton McCann Jr. "The Book of Psalms," in *The New Interpreter's Bible*, vol. 4, ed. Leander Keck (Nashville: Abingdon Press, 1996), 645.

Either way, this identification of worshipers is important. Normally those who are dead or slipping into death are not able to praise God (Psalm 6:5). But here even they are not outside the saving work of God and thus give praise.

## The Church: Offering Opportunity for Lament

What does it mean for the church that Jesus prayed Psalm 22? What does it teach us about Jesus? What does it teach us about our own life of prayer?

For starters, if Jesus prayed out of a feeling of God-forsakenness, it would seem the church should not hesitate to teach and practice a similar kind of prayer. We should recognize, however, that "teaching" and "practicing" such prayer imply hard and intentional work to inculcate a life of prayer that resembles what we encounter in Psalm 22. Worship leaders might model such prayer during weekly worship services, but the foundation for this type of praying may best be laid in Bible studies and prayer-group meetings. It is easy and tempting to reduce lament to griping about petty matters. So it is crucial to have time for instruction and reflection on what this type of prayer looks like and how Jesus models it for us.

One passage that might guide a group in learning to include lament in prayer is Hebrews 5:7, which describes Jesus' prayers: "In the days of his flesh, Jesus offered up prayers and supplications, with loud cries and tears, to the one who was able to save him from death, and he was heard because of his reverent submission." The writer of Hebrews does not focus on what Jesus prays for but on how Jesus relates to God. Jesus prayed in faith, with "supplication" and in "reverent submission." Supplication refers to humble petition. Reverent submission implies that Jesus prayed to discover and commit himself to God's will (see Mark 14:32–42). It is crucial that the church teaches prayer as an act of practicing obedience in faith. When we pray out of a sense of obedience, then we understand that our prayers bring us closer to God; in prayer we therefore work to discern God's purpose for us. Faith that God is for us and is working to bring goodness and peace to the world is the reason we go to God in prayer in the first place.

With this understanding of prayer as an act of obedience in faith, the church can offer petitions and even complain bitterly over the circumstances of life. This understanding of prayer sets our laments in proper context. Indeed, even the starkest complaint ("Why have you forsaken me?") does not express doubt that God is for us if prayed in faith. The church invites people to lament with assurance that God hears and that God cares about their needs.

Lament takes on a significance that is larger than any one person's personal issues and circumstances. The one who prays enters into solidarity with all those who suffer. So our laments are not narrow and merely personal complaints; instead, they reach out to God for the sake of others. Lament invites those who pray to join others who give testimony to God's ultimate victory over sin and death (see Psalm 22:25–31).

## For Reflection and Action

1. Reflect on a time when you felt abandoned by God. Why did you feel that way? What were the circumstances? What helped you through the experience? Share with your class how your faith changed as a result. How would you talk about God's work in your life during that dark time?

2. The psalmist calls God "my God," but the psalmist knows God from what God did in the past with Israel's ancestors. In what ways can you identify your own relationship with the God who led and guided the church in the past?

3. What are the benefits of giving testimony to God's deliverance as the psalmist does in Ps. 22:22–31?

4. How would you describe your relationship with God? How does the character of that relationship inform your prayer life?

*The role of humankind in God's creation is sufficiently complex, and we should not be surprised to find two psalms that present that role in separate ways.*

## Chapter 5

# Humans, Made a Little Lower than God

**Psalm 8** The psalm presents the human being as one made in God's image and as one who has a prominent place in God's sovereign reign over the universe.

**Psalm 104** This psalm complements Psalm 8 by presenting the human being as one of God's creatures, thus connoting the smallness of humanity in the larger creation.

## Prayer

O marvelous and wonder-working God, we marvel at the beauty of the earth and the vastness of space. We see your handiwork in the order and majesty of creation. Every land form, every color, every sound testifies to your sovereignty. In the totality of all you have made, we are so small. So we are humbled by the power you have given us to make peace, to reconcile people in conflict, and to love one another. Help us to live into our calling to be your agents for good on earth. In the name of Jesus, we pray. Amen.

## Introduction

What does it mean to be human? What place does God intend humans to have in creation? Scripture begins to address these questions in the very first chapter of the Bible. Genesis 1:26–27 says humans are made in the image of God. This means in part that they represent God in the work to bring about God's purpose in the creation. God gave humans the responsibility to finish the work of ordering the world. This is what it means for humans to "have dominion" and "subdue" the earth (Genesis 1:26, 28).

The Psalms deal with the question of human identity and purpose as well. The two psalms at the heart of this chapter speak to this subject directly. Psalms 8 and 104 give pictures of humans as central figures in God's creation.

Psalms 8 and 104 are hymns of praise. They testify to the truth that we understand the role and importance of humans only in relation to the reign of God. Both psalms begin and end by calling humans to praise (Psalms 8:1, 9; 104:1a, 35b). Between the expressions of praise both psalms celebrate the creation. Psalm 8 expresses wonder at God's creative power and at the magnificence of the creation itself. The heavens, the moon, the stars (Psalm 8:3), and even the babbling of babies (Psalm 8:2) testify to God's greatness.

Psalm 104 goes into greater detail than Psalm 8 about the nature of the world God made. The elaborate description of the order of the creation, in turn, is the medium by which the psalmist presents God's sovereignty and the human place in creation. In both psalms creation gives reason to stand in awe of God. Nevertheless, the two psalms emphasize humanity's role in strikingly different ways. Psalm 104 does not explicitly set humans apart from the rest of the creatures God made. They are simply part of the created order and have their place alongside domestic and wild animals, fish, and birds. In Psalm 8, however, humans are "a little lower than God." The psalm thus presents humans most clearly as those made in God's image.

## A Basic Theme: Humans, Made a Little Lower than God

Psalm 8:3–4 focuses on human beings and their place in the created order. The psalmist presents the high place of humans in creation as a marvel in the face of the magnificence of the rest of God's work. The question "What are humans?" has two notable features that are keys to the meaning of the psalm.

> *The reference to humankind here implies the weakness of the creature.* The word "human" translates the Hebrew *enosh*, a word that in the Psalms often refers to an impotent being (Psalms

9:20; 90:3; 103:15). The parallel expression *ben adam* (literally "son of man") likewise connotes the frailty of the human. The word *adam* derives from the same Hebrew root as the word for earth or soil (*adamah*; Genesis 2:7). The human is from the earth, not from the heavens.

*The question "What are humans?" puts the human in relation to God's greatness: "What are human beings that you are mindful of them?"* It is not an abstract query about the nature and identity of humankind. The verb in this case might be translated "remember" as it is in other contexts (*zakar*; see Genesis 8:1). God's "remembering" refers to God's keeping relationship. When the psalmist complains that God has forgotten (as in Psalm 13:1), the complaint is essentially that God has broken relationship. Psalm 8:4 assumes, however, that God's remembering is typical and expected, though undeserved.

Despite the frailty of human beings, verse 5 declares that God made them "a little lower than God." The word translated "God" is a general word (*elohim*) that may simply refer to divine beings such as angels or members of God's heavenly court. In Psalm 8 it is impossible to tell which is intended. The point, however, is not so much the identity of *elohim* but that God gave humans a royal office in God's creation. God put humans in charge of the earth, and their dominion extends to all living creatures. The portrait of humans in this section is much like the one in Genesis 1:1–2:4a. The image of God bestowed on humans in Genesis 1:26–28 is defined by human dominion. So also Psalm 8 describes the unique place of humans in terms of their place over other creatures. In Egypt, Pharaoh was said to bear the image of God, which stood for the deity on earth. But Psalm 8, as does Genesis 1:1–2:4, presents all humans in the royal office. This may be due in part to the fact that kingship ended in Israel in 587 BCE. The role once reserved for the king was transferred to humankind. Glory and honor are words that apply typically to monarchs, but here they describe all human beings. Thus, Psalm 8 highlights the unique place humans have in God's creation. They oversee and care for the rest of the creatures God made.

## The Life of Faith: The Place of Human in the Creation

One of the basic questions our faith addresses is, what is our purpose on this planet? If Psalm 8 presents the human being as the crown of creation, Psalm 104 does the opposite. It describes the human as one animal among many in God's creation. If Psalm 8 speaks in the language of Genesis 1, Psalm 104 seems closer to the book of Job. When Job called out to God in his suffering, he asked for answers: Why has this happened to me (Job 3)? God addresses Job "out of the whirlwind" (Job 38:1). God does not explain the reason for Job's suffering. Instead, God suggests Job cannot understand his suffering because his view of the world is limited. God presents the cosmos as a mysterious realm that Job cannot understand. God takes Job on a tour of the cosmos by a series of questions, each one essentially asking, "Where were you when I laid the foundation of the earth?" (Job 38:4). God lets Job know that he was a small creature in the scope of the whole creation.

In a comparable way Psalm 104 takes us on a tour of the cosmos and names humans as one of the creatures God made. Verses 2b–9 describe how God ordered the world and made it a habitable place for all creatures. The main problem was the waters in the seas. Ancient people thought of them as a threat because they surrounded the earth (from their vantage point) and seemed endless and mysterious. God put them in place and established limits for them so they could not threaten life (see Genesis 1:1–10). Then verses 10–13 report how God brought forth springs and streams as a source of life. Verse 14 notes that this life-giving water made "the grass to grow for the cattle, and plants for people to use." God provides for domestic animals and humans, and remarkably humans do not seem to have a superior place in God's care. Verses 19–23 tell how God set up times and seasons, day and night. At night the predators of the forest come out to seek their prey (vv. 20–21). It is their time. But when the sun rises their "work" is done (v. 22). "Day" is the time for humans to go to their labor (v. 23). For every creature there is a time, and God provides what they need. In the rhythms of day and night and the seasons of the year, humans have time allotted like all creatures.

The rest of Psalm 104 only reinforces the smallness of humans. The human stands in awe of God's work as creator (v. 24). The mighty and mysterious Leviathan (the great sea monster) is not mysterious to God but is beyond the grasp of humans. Moreover, humans are like all other creatures in that they have life because God put the breath of life in them. When God takes it away, they die (vv. 27–30).

## The Church: Practicing Being Human in the Age of Ecological Crisis

If the church is to speak to the needs of our world today it must address the basic problem of how human beings threaten the health of the earth. The two psalms in this chapter are primary resources. These two psalms at once call us to take responsibility for the earth and conceive of humanity as small and insignificant. Actually the two ways of approaching the ecological crisis complement each other.

Psalm 8:4–8 presents humans with echoes of Genesis 1:26–30. God gives them "dominion" over all the works of God's hands, which means that all the animals of the earth are "under their feet." In other words, humans have a royal office in God's kingdom. We are "rulers" of the earth on God's behalf.

The problem is that "dominion" in Psalm 8 is easily misunderstood. Some read it as a declaration of humanity's divinely ordained dominance of the earth. They feel free, indeed compelled, to exploit the earth and its resources for their advancement and pleasure.[1] Many Christians have interpreted the Bible in this way, but they have not read the Bible closely enough! God as Creator, from Genesis 1 through the Bible, carefully and lovingly shapes the creation for good. God does not exploit it or use it for self-advancement. Moreover, God puts the first human in the Garden of Eden "to till it and keep it" (Genesis 2:15). That is, the human's role was to keep and protect, not to "use" or "abuse." Dominion, as Psalm 8 intends, is not exploitation and abuse but caring for, tending, and feeding. So the church has responsibility to practice care for the earth that preserves and protects it and its resources.

Given the temptation to misunderstand what it means for humans to have "dominion" over the earth, Psalm 104 is a good corrective. Psalm 104 suggests that, like the book of Job, humans are small and insignificant from God's point of view. The creation

1. See Lynn White Jr., "The Historical Roots of Our Ecological Crisis," *Science* 155 (1967), 1203–7.

is vast, its many creatures are beyond our awareness, and the workings of it all are beyond our grasp. The psalm invites us to decenter humans in our thoughts about the creation. It is helpful from time to time to do so, not just to perceive our smallness but also to see how our future is tied up with the future of all other creatures.

These two ways of understanding the place of humankind really do go together. Humanity's interconnectedness with the rest of creation reminds us of what is at stake as we exercise "dominion." Our place "a little lower than God" reminds us that, despite our smallness, we are the only creatures with the ability to reflect on it all. Indeed, of all the wondrous works of God, God gave only humans responsibility to care for the rest. This message is built into both Psalm 8 and Psalm 104. As both psalms begin and end with praise, they remind us that we exercise our role as caregivers of the earth as those who depend on God for our very being and that we have no dominion apart from the graciousness of God.

## For Reflection and Action

1. Draw a picture of the universe, and place yourself in the picture. Where did you locate yourself? How does that location identify your relationship with other creatures? How does it identify your relationship with God? How do Psalms 8 and 104 add to your understanding of your place in the cosmos?

2. What do you regularly see in the nonhuman world that you think is a sign of God's goodness to you?

3. What are three practical ways you can better fill the role of one "made a little lower than God" in your care for the rest of creation? How will you follow up on these ideas?

4. Because of the discoveries of modern science, there is so much less mystery about the creation for us than for the psalmist. How do you think this increased understanding of the universe affects the way we think about our relationship to God and to the creation?

*The psalm in this chapter is one of the most difficult passages in the Bible. The final line rightly offends most readers, and some will not be able to accept it as part of Scripture.*

## Chapter 6

# Praying Anger

**Psalm 137**   This psalm has a bitter protest over the destruction of Jerusalem and a petition for God to bring justice to those who destroyed it.

## Prayer

O God, so much makes us angry, but much of our anger is petty. We seethe when someone cuts us off in traffic. We boil inside when we learn someone has spoken ill of us. Redirect our anger toward what really matters. Help us to see the evil in the world and to direct our prayers toward those who suffer from it. Be with all the victims of abuse, those who live in places torn apart by war, and those whose lives are at risk because of disease, famine, and poverty. Bring your justice for their sakes. In the name of Jesus we pray. Amen.

## Introduction

Most Christians do not learn to complain when they pray, much less to express anger. Yet, as we saw in chapter 2, if we read the prayers of the Psalter as model prayers, we learn that it is right and good to take all our emotions—our fears, our anxiety, and even our anger—to God. In this chapter we focus on a psalm that pushes that idea to its limits. Psalm 137 expresses grief and anger over the loss of Jerusalem, which the psalmist describes as "my highest joy" (v. 6). The psalmist anguishes over the Babylonian exile. In 587

BCE King Nebuchadnezzar of Babylon destroyed Jerusalem and its temple and took Judah's leading citizens into exile. The even radically disrupted life for the people of Judah and Jerusalem. The Babylonians effectively ended the Davidic monarchy that had ruled in Jerusalem for over four hundred years and destroyed the place of worship that had been their spiritual center. Psalm 137 is a gut-wrenching protest against what the Babylonians did to the people of Judah.

Psalm 137 poses two main problems for Christian theology especially as we consider how it might serve as a model prayer: (1) The psalmist prays against the enemy, which seems at odds with Jesus' instructions to forgive (Matthew 6:12) and to love enemies and to pray for them (Matthew 5:43–48). (2) This psalm ends (vv 7–9) with violent imagery, and it promotes violence against others So the primary questions are, Can we read Psalm 137 as part of Christian Scripture, and can it serve as an example of Christian prayer?

As we prepare to address these questions, it is important to remember that the church traditionally has read psalms like Psalm 137 not only as integral parts of Scripture but as consistent with the prayers and concerns of Jesus. This is possible when we recognize that the enemies in these psalms "are enemies of the cause of God" and not our personal enemies.[1] We will return to this point in the concluding section of the chapter.

## A Basic Theme: Anger at Loss and Injustice

In Psalm 137:1–6 the psalmist reveals the circumstances that gave rise to the psalm and expresses the pain that results from those circumstances. Verse 1 states the problem succinctly: "By the rivers of Babylon—there we sat down and there we wept when we remembered Zion." The psalmist is one of the exiles. "Rivers of Babylon" may refer to the Tigris and Euphrates, or it may connote the river Chebar, which was the location of Judah's settlement in exile (see Ezekiel 1:1). Regardless of the exact reference, verses 1–4 express pain at being far from home and removed from the source of life that Israelites found on Mount Zion.

Zion appears in verse 1 as a synonym for Jerusalem, but in

1. Dietrich Bonhoeffer, *Psalms: The Prayer Book of the Bible,* trans. James H. Burtness (Minneapolis: Augsburg Publishing House, 1970), 57.

some passages, it refers more narrowly to the hilltop in Jerusalem that King David chose as the temple's location (1 Kings 8:1; Psalm 132:13–16). Jerusalem was the seat of government; for the psalmist, the loss of Jerusalem was most important because it included the loss of Zion and the place of worship. The people of Judah believed Zion was the center of God's creation, the place from which God ruled over the world (see Psalm 2:6; 76:1–3).

Adding to the pain over the loss of Zion, the Babylonians taunted the exiles, saying, "'Sing us one of the songs of Zion!'" (v. 3). "Songs of Zion" refer to certain psalms that praise the beauty of Zion and celebrate God's choice of Zion as God's dwelling place (Psalms 46; 48; 76; 84; 87; 122). These psalms express the psalmist's longing for the temple and for the blessings of God they received by being there. Psalm 84:10 says, "For a day in your courts is better than an thousand elsewhere." The Babylonian captors mocked the Israelites' love for Zion and their faith in the God they worshiped in its temple.

The person who speaks for the exiles in Psalm 137 may be one of the Levites who made music in the temple and thus had intimate knowledge of the place and a supreme investment in its worship (see 1 Chronicles 16:4–6). The opening lament over being in a foreign land includes a reference to stringed instruments played in the temple: "On the willows there we hung up our harps" (v. 2). At the time of the writing of the psalm there is no music, nor can there be because there is no place to perform it. In the second section of the psalm (vv. 5–6) the psalmist alludes to making music as part of a pledge never to forget Jerusalem. "Let my right hand wither" (v. 5) probably means "Let me never play the harp again." The reference to the tongue (v. 6) probably has temple singing in mind. Hence, the psalmist expresses love for the holy city and its temple in what amounts to a self-curse: If I forget Jerusalem, let all my musical talents wither away, for Jerusalem is my highest joy (v. 6).

## The Life of Faith: Giving Anger to God

It is natural to be angry when one is the victim of injustice or when someone takes away something precious. The question then is, what do we do with our anger? Many readers identify with the grief-filled beginning of the psalm (vv. 1–6) but reject the final three verses because of their extremely angry rhetoric. Verse 7 asks God to remember against Edom. The Edomites cheered on the Babylonians when they attacked Jerusalem. Edom was Israel's "brother" (see Genesis 25:19–28), thus heir to the promises to Israel, and should understand the importance of Jerusalem for the stability of the world.

Verses 8 and 9 speak to Babylon directly. Babylon is called "devastator" because it destroyed Jerusalem (v. 8a). The psalm concludes with two beatitudes that address Babylon with some of the most shocking lines in the Bible:

> Happy shall they be who pay you
> back what you have done to us!

> Happy shall they be who take your little ones
> and dash them against the rock! (vv. 8b–9)

The last line seems to go beyond anything Christians would consider acceptable theologically or ethically. As we noted in chapter 1, the pronouncement "happy" suggests God's approval of the action described. How can anyone say that God would approve or reward someone who hurts "little ones"? When the Babylonians destroyed Jerusalem in 587 BCE, they killed the two sons of king Zedekiah to prevent a resurgence of the Davidic empire (2 Kings 25:7). The final line of Psalm 137 may well have been influenced by the experience of seeing Jerusalem's children dashed against the rocks. But regardless of the actions of the Babylonian army, surely, we could never say God promotes harm to children.

Three points may help us understand verses 7–9 and to see how these verses may inform our faith.

*Verses 8–9 are not addressed to God.* The psalmist addresses them to Babylon, as though the Babylonians would listen! The statements grow out of anger over Babylon's violent conquest of Jerusalem, but they do not actually ask God to do Babylon harm.

*The Edomites and the Babylonians appear in the Old Testament as primary examples of nations that oppose God's work in the world (see*

*Isaiah 47:1; Jeremiah 50:42; Psalm 2:1–6).* The psalmist indicts the nations because they imagined themselves to be in control of the world and its historical trajectory (see Habakkuk 1). The psalmist trusted that God would put Edom and Babylon in their place. This does not remove the difficulty of the language in verse 9, but it may be helpful to read the emotion-filled words as the psalmist's prayer for the Babylonian tyranny not to continue.

*Those who speak the words of verses 8–9 are not asking for power to retaliate.* Rather, they plead with God to remember against Edom, and they speak (rhetorically) against Babylon. That means then that the prayer to God in these verses is offered instead of acts of violence. It places the request for justice in the hands of God, where it belongs.

## The Church: Offering Prayers for Justice

The church is charged with encouraging a life of prayer that helps the one who prays develop a deeper relationship with God and a wider awareness of the needs of the world. One obstacle to that kind of faithful praying is the commonly held notion that prayer should be free of anger and frustration. It should be "nice." How does the church pray in the wake of trauma and injustice? Events like 9/11 and the shooting at a Pittsburgh synagogue on October 27, 2018, pose challenges for prayer. How should the church pray in response to such acts?

This question exposes the need for congregations to deepen their understanding of Christian prayer and the resources that inform it. The most obvious resource is the Lord's Prayer, but most of us miss how radical a prayer it is. When we take seriously the petition for God's kingdom to come on earth (Matthew 5:10), then we recognize that much of the prayer is a prayer for justice. An effort to understand this prayer more fully might include a class that studies a treatment of the prayer like John Dominic Crossan's book *The Greatest Prayer: Rediscovering the Revolutionary Message of the Lord's Prayer.*[2]

Recognizing the justice orientation of the Lord's Prayer helps us see more clearly that Jesus regularly acted to combat the evil

2. New York: HarperCollins, 2010.

he saw. Jesus is gentle, meek, and mild when dealing with people who are weak and vulnerable, but he shows strength against the oppressive forces at work against such people. The people of God rightly take part in Jesus' action against evil; prayer is a primary means for doing so.

Psalm 137 suggests two steps to praying against injustice:

*Acknowledge injustice in prayer.* Psalm 137 speaks of this with the word "remember." The psalmist remembers Zion, which has been lost. This kind of remembering is an act of resistance, for, as J. Clinton McCann says, for the victim of evil "to forget is to submit to evil."[3] When acts of violence or systems of injustice take away something or someone important, Psalm 137 suggests it is proper to remember that in prayer.

*Pray for God to act against injustice.* Psalm 137 asks God to "remember against" those who destroyed Zion. This is the part of praying about anger, however, that is most easily misused. As we lead and teach this kind of prayer, we must be careful not to allow prayer to become a forum in which we simply complain about personal grudges and petty injustices and ask God to act against those who have slighted us. One way to prevent that from happening is to foster a practice of praying for the needs of the poor, the homeless, and the oppressed in our communities and around the world.

## For Reflection and Action

1. Name a group of people who currently suffer injustice because of their racial, political, or religious identity or some other identifying characteristic. Then write a prayer for God to bring justice and equity to them. Include in your prayer a description of the wrongs they suffer and a petition for God to act for them.

2. In Psalm 137 the psalmist remembers Zion, the place of worship where God's people experienced God's presence. Have you ever lost something that important to you?

---

3. "The Book of Psalms," in *The New Interpreter's Bible,* vol. 4, ed. Leander Keck (Nashville: Abingdon Press), 1228.

3. In the psalm and in the Old Testament, Edom and Babylon represent those forces that try to undo the goodness of God. What are Edom and Babylon in your life?


4. How do you relate the anger Psalm 137 expresses to the New Testament injunction "Be angry but do not sin; do not let the sun go down on your anger, and do not make room for the devil" (Ephesians 4:26–27)?

# Group Gatherings

Eva Stimson

# The Meaning of Happiness

## Main Idea

The Hebrew word translated "happy" refers to the kind of life that God approves. The placement of Psalms 1 and 2 at the beginning of the Psalter invites readers to consider what "happy" really means.

## Preparing to Lead

- Read and reflect on chapter 1, "The Meaning of Happiness."
- Review this plan for the group gathering, and select questions and activities that you will use.
- Gather newsprint and markers, if needed, and prepare to post newsprint sheets on a wall or bulletin board.
- Preview the suggested scene from *Inside Out* (2015). Plan to show it to the group.
- What other questions, issues, or themes occur to you from your reflection?

## Gathering

- Provide name tags and pens as people arrive.
- Provide simple refreshments; ask volunteers to bring refreshments for the next five gatherings.
- Agree on simple ground rules and organization (for example, time to begin and end; location for gatherings; welcoming of all points of view; confidentiality; and so on). Encourage participants to bring their study books and Bibles.

## Opening Worship
### Prayer (unison)

O God, teach us the way to true happiness. Lead us to the waters that satisfy, to those that flow from your presence. Plant us near

43

you that you may nurture us and teach us your way, for we know that your way is the way to life. Lead us away from actions, activities, and words that are deceitful and destructive. Set us on the path Jesus walks, for we know that he will lead us to a life that is abundant and full. In the name of Jesus, who followed you perfectly, we pray. Amen.

## Prayerful, Reflective Reading

- Read Psalm 1 aloud.
- Invite all to reflect for a few minutes in silence.
- After reflection time, invite all to listen for a word or phrase as the passage is read again and to reflect on that word or phrase in silence.
- Read the passage a third time, asking all to offer a silent prayer following the reading.
- Invite volunteers to share the word or phrase that spoke most deeply to them.

## Prayer

Loving God, hear our prayers today as we seek to follow you more faithfully:

(*spoken prayers may be offered*)

Hear us now as we pray together, saying, Our Father . . .

## Conversation

- Introduce chapter 1, "The Meaning of Happiness." Share observations, reflections, and insights.
- Review some of the characteristics of the Psalms:
  a. Psalms in Hebrew is *tehellim*—meaning "praises." Psalms in Greek is *psalmoi*—referring to "songs accompanied by stringed instruments." Notice the format of the printed words; the Psalms are lyrics to songs.
  b. A particular tune for the words is often provided. What is the tune given "To the Leader" in Psalm 47? Discover the hymn tune for one of the following psalms: Psalm 7, Psalm 8, Psalm 9, Psalm 22, Psalm 45, or Psalm 75.
  c. Directions are often given. Notice the Hebrew word *selah* (for example, after Psalm 3). Some suggest it means "pause," others suggest "intensify," but its meaning is unknown.

d. The 150 psalms have been collected into five sections. Each section ends with a doxology—"Praise the Lord!" Read one of the doxologies: Psalm 41:13, Psalm 72:19, Psalm 89:52, Psalm 106:48, or Psalm 150:6.

e. Many of the psalms are linked to a particular event. Discover the event in one of the following psalms: Psalm 3, Psalm 18, Psalm 54, or Psalm 56.

f. The psalmists address God in several ways. Many of the psalms use the title "Lord." Discover one or more additional names for God in the following psalms: Psalm 4, Psalm 8, Psalm 9, Psalm 20, Psalm 47, Psalm 80, and Psalm 84.

- Review "A Basic Theme: Happiness as Dependence on God" (pp. 2–4). Share these key points:

a. "Happy" is the first word in Psalm 1 and thus the first word in the Psalter. It holds together the first two psalms (Psalms 1:1; 2:12) and therefore plays a significant role in the introduction to the Psalter.

b. Although "happy" may not be the best translation of the Hebrew word ("blessed" may be better), it is useful in engaging us in conversation about what we seek after and what we think brings contentment.

c. Happiness according to the Psalms is a state of being that results from closeness to God and obedience to God's will.

d. In Psalm 1 and elsewhere "happy" describes a group of people called "the righteous" as opposed to the "wicked."

- Ask participants to find one or more of the following verses in their Bibles: Psalm 1:1; 2:12; 33:12; 40:4; 41:1; 84:5; 94:12; 106:3; 112:1; 119:1; 119:2; 146:5. Have them read their verses (they don't have to be read in order). Explain that these verses are beatitudes (blessings), just like those spoken by Jesus to the crowd in the Sermon on the Mount. Discuss:

*How do these compare with what is generally understood to bring happiness?*

*Which translation do you prefer, "happy" or "blessed"? Why?*

*Do you agree with Dr. Creach that "to be happy is to be humble, vulnerable, and dependent on God"? Whom would you call "happy"? Why would you apply that label to him or her. Would you also describe that person as "righteous"? Why?*

- Review "The Life of Faith: Meditating on the Law as a Way to Happiness" (pp. 4–5). Share these key points:
  a. Most conceptions of happiness in our culture are tied to what a person owns or does.
  b. In the Psalms, however, happiness is determined by the degree to which a person relies on God to shape his or her life.
  c. Psalm 1 declares that the primary instrument of that divine shaping is "the law of the LORD" (v. 2). Psalm 1 says that the righteous find life's fulfillment in torah because torah points to the Lord's purpose for the world.
- Discuss:

  *What would "meditating" on God's word look like for you?*

  *What can you do to keep the words and truth of Scripture always in your mind and heart?*

- Lead the group in considering the ways we form pathways for our faith by recurring readings of Scripture, by memorizing a psalm, by learning a statement of faith, by repeating a prayer, and by singing a hymn. Direct the group to repeat Psalm 25:4—"Make me to know your ways, O LORD; teach me your paths." Repeat the phrase several times. Challenge the participants to repeat the verse throughout the week.
- Review "The Church: Proclaim Jesus Christ, the Happy Man" (pp. 5–6). Share these key points:
  a. The church has a significant challenge to define happiness as the Psalms do since so many definitions of happiness in our culture are based on materialism and consumerism.
  b. It can model this happiness as it works to fulfill its mission to the poor and suffering people of the world.
  c. When the church ministers to those who are suffering, it does so because it recognizes the need for partnership with the poor because Scripture recognizes the poor as "blessed" or "happy" (Luke 6:20; Matthew 5:3).

- Discuss:

*What do you think of the claim that Jesus is the quintessential happy man, using the description of happy in this chapter?*

*Mr. Rogers cherished the boy's prayers for, as he said, "I think that anyone who has gone through challenges like that must be very close to God." What Scripture passages speak about being close to God as a blessing? (Hint: Numbers 6:24–26.) Do you agree that enduring suffering draws God close?*

*If "poor" is a positive term that refers to those who depend on God, who are the poor in your world?*

*How does your church emphasize the importance of partnering with the poor in its outreach? If it doesn't, what can you do to bring attention to this?*

- Briefly, introduce the plot of the movie *Inside Out,* which tells the story of Riley from birth through childhood. The emotions of joy, sadness, fear, disgust, and anger guide her actions. Show a brief scene from the movie that portrays Riley's birth. We are introduced to the five forces guiding her life and to the islands of her personality: Goofball Island, Friendship Island, Honesty Island, and Family Island (start cue: 2:06, "Riley is born"; end cue: 7:19, "She's 11 now"). Discuss:

*In what ways do you recognize the five emotions—joy, sadness, anger, disgust, and fear—at work in your life? Does the absence of some emotions—such as love—surprise you?*

*If* Inside Out *was your story, what would be the primary islands of your personality?*

*How would you illustrate "Happiness Island?" What images would you add to express the Christian faith as living a life that God approves?*

## Conclusion

In his book *Wishful Thinking: A Theological ABC*, Frederick Buechner offers a connection between happiness and the needs of the world. Reflect on happiness and your vocation:

Vocation. It comes from the Latin *vocare*, to call, and means the work a man is called to by God. There are all different kinds of voices calling you to all different kinds of work, and the problem is to find out which is the voice of God rather than of Society, say, or the Superego, or Self-Interest. By and large a good rule for finding out is this. The kind of work God usually calls you to is the kind of work (a) that you most need to do and (b) that the world most needs to have done. . . . the place God calls you to is the place where your deep gladness and the world's deep hunger meet.[1]

## Passing the Peace

The peace of Christ be with you.
    And also with you.
**Amen.**

1. Frederick Buechner, *Wishful Thinking: A Theological ABC* (San Francisco: HarperSanFrancisco, 1973), 95.

# The Lord Is My Shepherd

## Main Idea

"I shall not want" challenges our natural inclinations to desire and seek after so many things, and it draws our attention to God's provision of what matters most.

## Preparing to Lead

- Read and reflect on chapter 2, "The Lord Is My Shepherd."
- Review this plan for the group gathering, and select questions and activities that you will use.
- Gather newsprint and markers, if needed, and prepare to post newsprint sheets on a wall or bulletin board.
- Prepare to read the Hebrew version of Psalm 23 phonetically. Or play the entire psalm spoken or sung in Hebrew from a recording. Search the Internet for "Psalm 23 in Hebrew," and multiple options will be provided.
- Secure a recording of "Shepherd" by Todd Agnew. Prepare to play it for the group.
- What other questions, issues, or themes occur to you from your reflection?

## Gathering

- Provide simple refreshments as people arrive and name tags if needed.

## Opening Worship
**Prayer** (unison)

Eternal God, you led your people Israel through the wilderness, and you carried them like little lambs when they were far from home. We know that you have carried us also. From birth you have watched over us and nurtured us with your love. May we now submit to your shepherding care that you may lead us to the waters that satisfy and to pastures where you feed us. Remind us that as you direct our paths toward righteousness, you prepare us for the dark valleys we inevitably travel, and that in them we are never alone. In the name of Jesus our shepherd, we pray. Amen.

## Prayerful, Reflective Reading

- Read Psalm 23 and 100 aloud responsively as best suits your group.

23:1    The LORD is my shepherd, I shall not want.

**100:1    Make a joyful noise to the LORD, all the earth.**

23:2    He makes me lie down in green pastures; he leads me beside still waters;

**100:2    Worship the LORD with gladness; come into his presence with singing.**

23:3    he restores my soul. He leads me in right paths for his name's sake.

**100:3    Know that the LORD is God. It is he that made us, and we are his; we are his people, and the sheep of his pasture.**

23:4    Even though I walk through the darkest valley, I fear no evil; for you are with me; your rod and your staff—they comfort me.

**100:4    Enter his gates with thanksgiving, and his courts with praise. Give thanks to him, bless his name.**

23:5    You prepare a table before me in the presence of my enemies; you anoint my head with oil; my cup overflows.

**100:5    For the LORD is good; his steadfast love endures forever, and his faithfulness to all generations.**

23:6    Surely goodness and mercy shall follow me all the days of my life, and I shall dwell in the house of the LORD my whole life long.

- Invite all to reflect for a few minutes in silence, asking all to offer a silent prayer following the reading.
- Invite volunteers to share their feelings and thoughts about the reading. What do Psalms 23 and 100 tell us about the Lord our shepherd?

## Prayer

Loving God, hear our prayers today as we seek to follow you more faithfully:

(*spoken prayers may be offered*)

Hear us now as we pray together, saying, Our Father . . .

## Conversation

- Introduce chapter 2, "The Lord Is My Shepherd." Share observations, reflections, and insights.
- Review the Introduction (pp. 9–10). Share these key points:
  a. The image of God as shepherd is one of the most popular in all of Scripture undoubtedly because it offers comfort for people in trouble.
  b. Psalm 23 speaks to all times in life, not just at funerals or during times of loss.
  c. It draws our attention to God's provision of what matters most.
- Listen to the language of the Psalms by reading the opening verses of Psalm 23 in Hebrew.
  *Adonai Ro'i, lo echsar*—The Lord is my shepherd, I shall not want.
  *Bin'ot desche yarbitzeini*—he makes me lie down in green pastures;
  *`al-mei menuchot yenahaleini*—he leads me beside still waters;
  *nafshi yeshoveiv*—he restores my soul.
  Sound out the following phonetic pronunciation of the Hebrew:
  Ah-don-eye row-ee, lo eksar
  Bin-ote desh-ay yar-bit-zany
  ahl-may men-ook-ote yeh-nock-ah-lany
  noff-she yesh-oh-vave.
- Review "A Basic Theme: The Lord Is My Shepherd" (pp. 10–11). Share these key points:
  a. God cares for the psalmist as a shepherd cares for sheep. Just as sheep depend on the shepherd to find food and water and to live free of life-threatening circumstances, so the psalmist relies on the Lord.

b. The Jewish people were surrounded by other nation who were ruled by tyrants and who worshiped gods tha were believed to act capriciously for their own benefit. By contrast, God's people believed that kings were meant to be shepherds, not despots. In this they were following a divine model: God cares for the people as a shepherd cares for sheep.

c. Psalm 23, attributed to David, is the best-known expres sion of this kingship model in the Old Testament.

d. Another image appears in verse 5, namely, God as host This image comes from the ancient practice of hospitality

- Invite learners to look again at Psalm 23. Tell the group tha the psalm is full of "Godverbs." A Godverb is a part of speech that describes the things God does. Form teams, and hand out paper and pencils. Ask teams to dig into the psalm and write down all the phrases they can find that contain God verbs. When groups have finished, invite each to share one Godverb phrase at a time. Have the next group share a phrase and so on until the list is complete.

- Discuss:

   *What do these Godverbs tell us about God?*

   *When have you experienced one or more of these Godverbs in your own life?*

   *Psalm 23 expands the image of God as shepherd by also including the image of God as host. How does God "host" us? What kind of protection and comfort does God give?*

   *Which metaphors from contemporary life speak of protection and comfort? First responders? Therapists? How does it feel to say, "The Lord is my first responder"?*

- Review "The Life of Faith: God as Shepherd in a Consumer Culture" (pp. 11–13). Share these key points:

   a. One of the most remarkable claims of Psalm 23 comes in the statement that follows the opening metaphor: "I shall not want" (v. 1b), which has been misinterpreted.

b. Misinterpretation 1. A relationship with the divine shepherd causes us to reorganize our priorities and want little.
c. Misinterpretation 2. God gives us all the material riches we want.
- Discuss:

> Dr. Creach writes, "So, what does the psalmist mean by 'I shall not want?' The answer seems to lie in the psalmist's recognition that God's presence is the most valuable blessing any person can have. It does not deny the need and desire for food, safety, and material goods, but they all take second place to God's presence."
>
> Is God's presence the most valuable thing in your life? Why?
>
> How do you seek the Lord's face or presence in your life?
>
> The ultimate destination for the psalmist is the "house of the LORD," which seems to refer to the place of worship. In what ways have you found safety and guidance in a worshiping community?
>
> What does it mean to you that God leads you into "right paths?" How does God provide such leadership for you?

- Review "The Church: Proclaiming the Promises of God as Shepherd" (pp. 13–14). Share these key points:
  a. It is appropriate for the church to highlight this intimate portrait of a savior who protects and guides us through life. The picture essentially refutes the idea of a clockmaker God who is removed from the daily challenges of believers.
  b. To have God as shepherd means that God directs every aspect of life. Far from being removed from our circumstances, Psalm 23 declares that the divine shepherd is near to us in even the darkest valleys.
  c. "Shepherd" implies authority. In the ancient world the shepherd image was popular with kings because people understood how the relationship between shepherd and sheep worked.

- Listen together to "Shepherd" by Todd Agnew. To help participants find connections between the song and Psalm 23, discuss the following:

> The first stanza describes people who are in really bad shape. In what ways do you connect with these words?

> The lyrics contrast people's wants and their needs. What desires leave us feeling hungry even when we satisfy them? In contrast, what are our real needs?

> Imagine a new final stanza that represents God's response. What might God say?

> In a world full of need, how can the church best proclaim the promise of God's goodness and mercy to those who need to hear it?

## Conclusion

Read John 10:16. Explain that the first sheep Jesus referred to were the Jews while the "other sheep" in this verse were probably the Gentiles. In our day, "other sheep" might be other Christians with whom we disagree or refuse to join at table. Christ our shepherd calls us to examine our attitudes, practices, and behaviors that keep us safe from the concerns and needs of Christ's other sheep. Discuss and commit to ways to reach out to someone in need this week.

## Passing the Peace

The peace of Christ be with you.
    And also with you.
**Amen.**

# Thirsting for God

## Main Idea

The Psalms express a longing for God's presence, which is better than anything else. The psalmist is far from home and far from the place of worship, the place that gives proper orientation to goodness and truth.

## Preparing to Lead

- Read and reflect on chapter 3, "Thirsting for God."
- Review this plan for the group session, and select questions and activities that you will use.
- Gather newsprint and markers, if needed, and prepare to post newsprint sheets on a wall or bulletin board.
- Prepare one of two options to show portions of the movie *Babette's Feast* (1988, directed by Gabriel Axel). Search streaming services for video clips and the full movie.
- What other questions, issues, or themes occur to you from your reflection?

## Gathering

- Provide simple refreshments as people arrive and name tags if needed.

## Opening Worship
### Prayer (unison)

Creator and Redeemer God, you alone can truly satisfy us. You made us in your love to have fellowship with you. When we rebelled against you, you sought us out and drew us back to yourself. Your steadfast love is better than life itself. Yet we often seek our identity and our fulfillment in short-term pleasures our culture urges us to thirst after. Teach us again that we find our purpose only when we find ourselves in you. Remind us—we who want so much—that when we have you, we have everything we need. Amen.

## Prayerful, Reflective Reading

- Read Psalm 63 aloud.
- Invite all to reflect for a few minutes in silence.
- After reflection time, invite all to listen for a word or phrase as the passage is read again and to reflect on that word or phrase in silence.
- Read the passage a third time, asking all to offer a silent prayer following the reading.
- Invite volunteers to share the word or phrase that spoke most deeply to them.

## Prayer

Loving God, hear our prayers today as we seek to follow you more faithfully:

(*spoken prayers may be offered*)

Hear us now as we pray together, saying, Our Father . . .

## Conversation

- Introduce chapter 3, "Thirsting for God." Share observations, reflections, and insights.
- Review "A Basic Theme: Thirsting for the Presence of God" (pp. 16–17). Share these key points:
  a. The psalms in this lesson are like Psalm 23 in that they express a longing for God's presence that is better than anything else.
  b. The image of "thirst" guides both psalms. In Psalm 42:1–2 water represents life, with God as the source. In Psalm 42:7 water becomes threatening, a symbol of trouble and despair. These threatening waters represent the psalmist's distress over God's absence.
  c. A primary issue in Psalms 42–43 and 63 is that the psalmist is far from home and the place of worship that gives proper orientation to goodness and truth.
- Invite participants to name all the Bible stories they can think of that include water. Some are listed here:

Creation—Genesis 1
Noah and the flood—Genesis 7
Crossing the Red Sea—Exodus 14
Water in the wilderness—Exodus 17:1–7
Crossing the Jordan—Joshua 3
The great river from the temple—Ezekiel 47:1–12
The waters of the womb—Luke 1:39–45
Jesus' baptism—Mark 1:9–11
Our baptism—Romans 6:3–4
The river of life—Revelation 22:1–6

Include the stories that group members don't name. Look up any obscure or unfamiliar stories and discuss them as you add them to the list. Ask the participants to determine which stories depict water as life and closeness to God and which depict water as threatening separateness from God.

• Discuss:

> *Can you remember a time when you were very thirsty? How did you feel? What would it be like if you couldn't just turn on the tap for some water to drink?*
>
> *When have you felt distant from God? Was it because God was far away? Or were you far away from God? What's the difference?*
>
> *Does "thirst" describe your disposition when you are far from God? If not, what image helps you speak about the feelings of being separated from God?*

• Review "The Life of Faith: The Living God as the One Who Satisfies Thirst" (pp. 17–18). Share these key points:
   a. We are constantly bombarded with advertising that suggests we need all sorts of things (and experiences), most of them being products the advertisers are selling: a new car, a certain food or drink, a line of clothing that gives a particular "look." It is easy to believe such messages because the commercials present images of success and satisfaction that seem compelling.

b. These material things do not satisfy our thirst for satisfaction at a deeper level. They merely give the illusion of success and contentment.

c. The psalmist thirsts for "the living God," a phrase that suggests God oversees life itself and is in charge of life, with power to give it or take it away.

d. The Israelites declared that the "living God," in contrast to other people's gods, did not simply make them richer in money and crops. Indeed, the living God entered into relationship with them, laid claim to their lives, and directed their lives toward goodness.

- Discuss:

> *How does the "living God" of Psalm 42 differ from popular ideas about God in contemporary culture?*

> *The greatest gift the living God gave was not crops but steadfast love (Hebrew* chesed). *"Steadfast love" is an Old Testament code for remembering the covenant with God. How is the covenant a gift to you?*

> *Have you ever felt that no one around you understood what your faith gives you? What is that experience like?*

- Review "The Church: Satisfying Thirst in the Gathering of Believers" (pp. 19–20). Share these key points:

a. Worship should give voice to the truth that the gospel is countercultural. What gives life is "not of this world," and those who embrace it are "resident aliens."

b. Part of the church's invitation to meet the living God should be an invitation to experience beauty. Psalm 27:4 speaks of a desire "to behold the beauty of the LORD."

c. Fellowship should go with worship. "My soul is satisfied as with a rich feast" (Psalm 63:5).

- Watch *Babette's Feast*, the story of a French servant woman named Babette who prepares a lavish French feast for members of a puritanical prayer group in an isolated Norwegian village in 1883. The feast transforms the lives of the little community through a faith-based appreciation for beauty.

Option 1: Watch the YouTube video *"Babette's Feast* Official Trailer."
Option 2: Find a three- to five-minute scene of the movie that shows the transformation among the community when they open their eyes to beauty.

- Discuss:

> Some movie viewers have seen the generous grace of God represented in the feast and make comparisons with the Eucharist (Lord's Supper). In what sense is your church's celebration of Communion a "feast"?

> According to the movie, how does beauty satisfy "thirst"?

> How is experiencing beauty an intentional part of your life and your congregation's life?

> How do you perceive people in your congregation satisfying a "thirst"?

> In what ways does beauty open your heart to the countercultural truth of God? To fellowship with God and fellow members of your church community?

## Conclusion

By becoming intentional and mindful in our seeing and listening, even in our tasting, touching, and smelling, we can heighten our attentiveness to the creation's beauty and God's glory. Challenge participants to practice new habits of mindfulness—prepare a meal from raw ingredients, and eat it slowly with good friends; pay attention to fresh flowers in bloom; greet neighbors; note rezoning proposals that may change the ecology of your neighborhood.

## Passing the Peace

The peace of Christ be with you.
    And also with you.
**Amen.**

# Praying to God for Help

## Main Idea

Jesus quoted from Psalm 22, and the Gospel writers used it to frame the passion because Jesus' suffering followed a typical pattern of the righteous sufferer in the Old Testament.

## Preparing to Lead

- Read and reflect on chapter 4, "Praying to God for Help."
- Review this plan for the group gathering, and select questions and activities that you will use.
- Gather newsprint and markers, and prepare to post newsprint sheets on a wall or bulletin board.
- On newsprint write the words, *My God, my God, why have you forsaken me?* Tape the paper to the wall.
- Call participants during the week, and ask them to bring music that speaks to them of despair. Suggest that they play the music on their smartphones.
- What other questions, issues, or themes occur to you from your reflection?

## Gathering

- Provide simple refreshments as people arrive and name tags if needed.

## Opening Worship

**Prayer** (unison)

O God, in Jesus Christ you have come and stood with us in the depths of pain and suffering. So we dare cry out to you with petitions for justice and cries for comfort, believing that you hear and answer us: attend the needs of those who are hungry, those who live with the threat of disease for themselves and for their children, the victims of discrimination and prejudice, and those who have suffered from floods, earthquakes, and other natural disasters. Attend our needs, O God, and make us instruments of your peace and healing. In the name of Jesus, we pray. Amen.

## Prayerful, Reflective Reading

- Invite the participants to take a moment and reflect on the phrase you have posted on the wall. Ask them to think of times when they have felt forsaken.
- Ask two volunteers to read from Matthew 27 and Psalm 22 according to the following order: Matthew 27:32–35; Psalm 22:16–18; Matthew 27:36–39a; Psalm 22:6–7; Matthew 27:40; Psalm 22:8; Matthew 27:43b, 45–46; Matthew 27:46b and Psalm 22:1a; Psalm 22:1–2; Psalm 22:14–15; and Matthew 27:50b–51.
- Invite all to reflect for a few minutes in silence.
- After reflection time, invite all to name ways that the reading surprised them.
- Praise God together for God's presence that carries you through dark times.

## Prayer

Loving God, hear our prayers today as we seek to follow you more faithfully:

(*spoken prayers may be offered*)

Hear us now as we pray together, saying, Our Father . . .

## Conversation

- Introduce chapter 4, "Praying to God for Help." Share observations, reflections, and insights.
- Review the Introduction (pp. 21–22). Share these key points:
  a. Psalm 22 is perhaps the most influential psalm for those who authored the story of Jesus' passion. The New Testament authors saw in this psalm a model for describing the Lord's suffering.
  b. Some people may struggle with the question of how Psalm 22 relates to the Gospel story. They may not be able to

see Psalm 22 apart from the passion narrative and read it essentially as a prediction of it.

c. Jesus quoted from Psalm 22, and the Gospel writers used it to frame the passion (especially Matthew and Mark) not because Psalm 22 predicted Jesus' suffering but because Jesus' suffering followed a typical pattern of the righteous sufferer in the Old Testament. This is the primary identity of David in Psalms (see Psalms 3 and 63 as examples). Thus, Jesus fulfills his role as "son of David" perfectly by praying Psalm 22:1.

- Invite someone to play a song that speaks of despair or of feeling lost and alone. Discuss:

  *What does the song say? What is the tone of the music?*

  *Do the music and the words "fit together"?*

  *Is it all bad news, or is there any word of hope in the lyrics?*

  *Is there a particular song you turn to when you're going through a challenging time?*

  *What promises in Scripture give you strength and courage during such times? Why?*

  *When do you find yourself humming a familiar hymn or remembering the words of a song sung in church?*

- Review "A Basic Theme: Complaining to God about Suffering" (pp. 22–23). Share these key points:
  a. Psalm 22 addresses God, describes the psalmist's trouble, and offers a plea for God to act.
  b. The opening question ("My God, my God, why have you forsaken me?") lets us know there is no restriction on what we can say to God.
  c. We can lay our souls bare before God. The psalm suggests God is not offended and perhaps even welcomes such bold prayer.

• Discuss:

*Reflect on a time when you felt abandoned by God. Why did you feel that way? What were the circumstances? What helped you through the experience? How would you talk about God's work in your life during that dark time?*

*How comfortable are you in complaining to God? Why?*

• Review "The Life of Faith: Out of Trouble Comes Praise" (pp. 23–25). Share these key points:
   a. In Jesus' day, faithful Jews learned the Scriptures by memorizing them. Jesus would have known the entire psalm, not just the first verse. So would his listeners. When Jesus cried out the first verse of a psalm, they would automatically "play" the entire psalm in their minds.
   b. Did Jesus really feel forsaken? Millions of Christians have found hope in their own despair by believing Jesus also felt despair. Unless he was truly human, they reason, he could never be our Savior and understand us. So it is important for their faith to believe that Jesus felt forsaken.
   c. Others need to believe that Jesus meant the entire psalm and was praising God. Their faith needs for Jesus to be truly God and for the relationship between the Father and Son to be unblemished by such a strong human feeling as despair.

• Discuss:

*As you reflect on Psalm 22 as the prayer Jesus prayed on the cross, what gives you hope in your troubles?*

*Dr. Creach maintains, "The power of Psalm 22 and the potential for it to serve as a model for us rests both in the extreme, unrestrained language of complaint and the sure faith with which the psalmist prays." Do you agree? Why?*

*The psalmist prays as one of God's people and, as such, as one who remembers God's faithfulness that elicited Israel's praise in ages past (v. 3). In what ways can you identify your* own relationship with God, who has led and guided the church through the centuries?

What are the benefits of giving testimony to God's deliverance as the psalmist does in Ps. 22:22–31?

- Form small groups to create new songs. Assign each of the groups one of four themes: help (Psalm 34:17–18); rescue (Psalm 37:39–40): heal (Psalm 30:1–2); and save (Psalm 69:1–3). Ask them to write a new psalm of at least four verses based on their assigned psalm excerpt and theme. Discuss:

  What may have caused the psalmist to cry out to God?

  What does the psalmist long for God to do?

  What do you long for? Help, rescue, healing, or salvation?

  How have you come to see God in such circumstances?

- Review "The Church: Offering Opportunity for Lament" (pp 25–26). Share these key points:
  a. If Jesus prayed out of a feeling of God-forsakenness, the church should not hesitate to teach and practice a similar kind of prayer.
  b. "Teaching" and "practicing" such prayer imply hard and intentional work to inculcate a life of prayer that resembles what we encounter in Psalm 22.
  c. Prayer is an act of practicing obedience in faith. When we pray out of a sense of obedience, then we understand that our prayers bring us closer to God; in prayer we therefore work to discern God's purpose for us.
- Discuss:

  How would you describe your relationship with God? How does the character of that relationship inform your prayer life?

  How would you describe your congregation's relationship with God? How does the character of that relationship inform your church's prayer life?

*When are you encouraged to offer prayers of lament or complaint in your church? Have there been tragic or troubling circumstances in the life of your church or community that found voice in prayers of complaint? Why? Why not?*

## Conclusion

Read Psalm 40:1–3, and invite the participants to enter into the emotions of the psalmist. Ask:

*What does the psalmist seek in crying out to God?*

*What is the new song the psalmist is singing?*

*What new song do you sing when God has heard your cries and delivered you from evil?*

## Passing the Peace

The peace of Christ be with you.
    And also with you.
Amen.

# Humans, Made a Little Lower than God

## Main Idea

Two complementary views of the place of humankind in God's creation are raised: an understanding of humans as special, made in God's image, and as one creature among many.

## Preparing to Lead

- Read and reflect on chapter 5, "Humans, Made a Little Lower than God."
- Review this plan for the group gathering, and select questions and activities that you will use.
- Gather newsprint and markers, if needed, and prepare to post newsprint sheets on a wall or bulletin board.
- Secure a video camera, or use a smartphone or tablet to record a video.
- What other questions, issues, or themes occur to you from your reflection?

## Gathering

- Provide simple refreshments as people arrive and name tags if needed.

## Opening Worship
**Prayer** (unison)

O marvelous and wonder-working God, we marvel at the beauty of the earth and the vastness of space. We see your handiwork in the order and majesty of creation. Every land form, every color, every sound testifies to your sovereignty. In the totality of all you have made, we are so small. So we are humbled by the power you have given us to make peace, to reconcile people in conflict, to love one another. Help us to live into our calling to be your agents for good on earth. In the name of Jesus, we pray. Amen.

## Prayerful, Reflective Reading

- Invite participants to turn to Psalm 8 and read the psalm silently.
- Then read it aloud together as a group, but in a quiet whisper.
- Finally, ask the group to read the psalm aloud one more time, starting with one voice and adding more voices with each verse, building into crescendo by the end.

## Prayer

Loving God, hear our prayers today as we seek to follow you more faithfully:

(*spoken prayers may be offered*)

Hear us now as we pray together, saying, Our Father . . .

## Conversation

- Introduce chapter 5, "Humans, Made a Little Lower than God." Share observations, reflections, and insights.
- Review the Introduction (pp. 27–28). Share these key points:
  a. Psalms 8 and 104 have complementary views of the place of humankind in God's creation. We need both an understanding of humans as special, made in God's image, and as one creature among many in order to grasp the place we occupy.
  b. Some participants may be troubled by the idea that the two passages do not speak with one voice. It may be helpful, however, to point out that we often express our theology as sets of tensions: Jesus Christ is human and divine; God is imminent and transcendent; God is Spirit, but God took on flesh.
  c. So also the role of humankind in God's creation is sufficiently complex, and we should not be surprised to find two psalms that present that role in diverse ways.
- Review "A Basic Theme: Humans, Made a Little Lower than God" (pp. 28–29). Share these key points:

a. Psalm 8 presents the human being as one made in God's image—humans are "a little lower than God"—and as one who has a prominent place in God's reign over the universe. Psalm 8's view of humanity is similar to that of the Genesis 1 creation story.

b. In Genesis 1:26–28 humans are God's final and highest creative act before resting and admiring the creation. Human beings are created in God's own image. The use of the word "image" may be a response to the Babylonian religion, where fixed images (idols) were common.

c. Both male and female are created simultaneously. They are given much, and much is expected of them.

• Discuss:

*What do you regularly see in the nonhuman world that you think is a sign of God's goodness to you?*

*How does it feel to be entrusted with the oversight of God's creation?*

*What things make it difficult to care for God's creation?*

*How do you feel about the responsibility human beings have for creation? If you were God, would you have given humans this much responsibility? Why or why not?*

*What are three practical ways you can better fill the role of one "made a little lower than God" in your care for the rest of creation? How will you follow up on these ideas?*

• Review "The Life of Faith: The Place of Human in the Creation" (pp. 30–31). Share these key points:

a. Psalm 104 presents the human being as one of God's creatures and thus connotes the smallness of humanity in the larger creation. Psalm 104's view of humanity is similar to that of the Genesis 2 creation story.

b. In Genesis 2, God's first creative act was to take dust from the ground (*'adamah*) and create a "man" (*'adam*) to till the as-yet-unmanaged earth (2:5–6).

c. God recognized that something was missing: "It is not good that the man should be alone" (2:18). So a process was begun to find a partner for the man that finally led to the creation of a woman from the rib of the man (2:23). Thereby a "helper," a helpmate, was provided to the man. The two together, and equally, tilled and cared for God's garden (2:21–23).

- Distribute paper and pencils. Ask the group members to draw a picture of the universe and place themselves in the picture. Discuss:

  *Where did you locate yourself?*

  *How does that location identify your relationship with other creatures?*

  *How does it identify your relationship with God?*

  *How do Psalms 8 and 104 add to your understanding of your place in the cosmos?*

- Review "The Church: Practicing Being Human in the Age of Ecological Crisis" (pp. 31–32). Share these key points:
  a. Psalms 8 and 104's ways of understanding the place of humankind go together. Humanity's interconnectedness with the rest of creation reminds us of what is at stake as we exercise "dominion." Our place "a little lower than God" reminds us that, despite our smallness, we are the only creatures with the ability to reflect on it all.
  b. "Dominion" has sometimes been interpreted as if the world exists solely for our pleasure so that we can use and abuse it as we please.
  c. In recent years, we have realized that we are not solely the monarchs of the earth and its creatures but the good stewards who provide for the health and well-being of a world where each created thing is precious and deserves to be cared for.

- On a sheet of newsprint, lead the group in rewriting Psalm 8:6 in their own words. The Hebrew word for "dominion" or "rule" is *radah*, which means "to exercise oversight." Basically, it means that God has entrusted humanity with the care of creation. Ask:

*Because of the discoveries of modern science, there is so much less mystery about the creation for us than for the psalmist. How do you think this increased understanding of the universe affects the way we think about our relationship to God and to the creation?*

*Take a moment to think of how you personally feel connected to or disconnected from the natural world. Where do you most clearly see God in creation? How do you best reflect the image of God in your own life?*

*How can the congregation carry out its calling to care for the creation, to exercise "dominion" in the sense of a care-taking responsibility?*

- Using a video camera, smartphone, or tablet, create a video that explains what Christians can do to care for God's creation. Lead the group in creating a short video that challenges other Christians to care for God's creation. Have the group choose a concept for the video, assign roles, and then record the video. Encourage the group to include why it's important for Christians to care for God's creation. Include specific things Christians can do to practice this care. If possible, upload the video to your congregation's website.

## Conclusion

Have participants organize a cleanup day for your congregation by adopting a road or community park that has an abundance of trash. During the experience, read one of the Scripture passages from this session aloud. Consider having participants plant native flowers and other plants during the experience. Discuss the possibility of making this an ongoing project for your congregation.

## Passing the Peace

The peace of Christ be with you.
    And also with you.
**Amen.**

# Praying Anger

## Main Idea

Psalm 137 calls us to reflect on our anger at injustice and connect with the kind of loss the psalmist experienced and the depth of anger over that loss.

## Preparing to Lead

- Read and reflect on chapter 6, "Praying Anger."
- Review this plan for the group gathering, and select questions and activities that you will use.
- Gather newsprint and markers, if needed, and prepare to post newsprint sheets on a wall or bulletin board.
- Preview and prepare to show the YouTube video *"He Named Me Malala* Official Trailer 1 (2015)."
- What other questions, issues, or themes occur to you from your reflection?

## Gathering

- Provide simple refreshments as people arrive and name tags if needed.

## Opening Worship

### Prayer (unison)

O God, so much makes us angry, but much of our anger is petty. We seethe when someone cuts us off in traffic. We boil inside when we learn someone has spoken ill of us. Redirect our anger toward what really matters. Help us to see the evil in the world and to direct our prayers toward those who suffer from it. Be with all the victims of abuse, those who live in places torn apart by war, and those whose lives are at risk because of disease, famine, and poverty. Bring your justice for their sakes. In the name of Jesus we pray. Amen.

## Prayerful, Reflective Reading

- Read Psalm 137 aloud.
- Invite all to reflect for a few minutes in silence.
- After reflection time, invite all to listen for a word or phrase a: the passage is read again and to reflect on that word or phrase in silence.
- Read the passage a third time, asking all to offer a silent prayer following the reading.
- Invite volunteers to share the word or phrase that spoke most deeply to them.

## Prayer

Loving God, hear our prayers today as we seek to follow you more faithfully:

(*spoken prayers may be offered*)

Hear us now as we pray together, saying, Our Father . . .

## Conversation

- Introduce chapter 6, "Praying Anger." Share observations reflections, and insights.
- Review the Introduction (pp. 33–34). Share these key points:
  a. The Babylonian exile constitutes the historical background of Psalm 137. In 587 BCE, the Babylonians destroyed Jerusalem and the temple and carried many Judean elites (the smartest and strongest) into captivity.
  b. Remembering is an important theme in Psalm 137. The psalm consists of three sections: vv. 1–4, 5–6, and 7–9. In each, a form of the Hebrew verb "to remember" (*zacar*) occurs (vv. 1, 6, and 7).
  c. Psalm 137 is one of the most difficult passages in the Bible. The final line rightly offends most readers, and some will not be able to accept it as part of Scripture.
- Review "A Basic Theme: Anger at Loss and Injustice" (pp. 34–35). Share these key points:
  a. Psalm 137 is a gut-wrenching protest against what the Babylonians did to the people of Judah.
  b. Psalm 137:1–4 expresses pain at being far from home and removed from the source of life that Israelites found on

Mount Zion. The loss of Jerusalem included the loss of the temple, the people's place of worship.

c. The Babylonians taunted the exiles by calling on them to "sing us one of the songs of Zion." This request conjures images of the minstrel shows that mocked former African American slaves in the late nineteenth and early twentieth centuries.

• Discuss:

*What makes you angry? What loss has angered you? What kinds of injustice anger you?*

*In Psalm 137 the psalmist remembers Zion, the place of worship where God's people experienced God's presence. Have you ever lost something that important to you?*

*What are some of the experiences of communal suffering that reach the level of pain the psalmist experiences (e.g., the suffering of Holocaust victims, the devastation of 9/11, and the suffering of Palestinians in occupied territories, Native Americans, and similar groups)? How would you express your anger if you had suffered in those circumstances?*

• Review "The Life of Faith: Giving Anger to God" (pp. 35–37). Share these key points to understand verses 7–9 and to see how these verses may inform our faith:

a. Verses 8–9 express anger over Babylon's violent conquest of Jerusalem, but they do not ask God to do Babylon harm.

b. The Edomites and the Babylonians are examples of nations that oppose God's work in the world. The psalmist trusted that God would put Edom and Babylon in their place.

c. Those who speak the words of verses 8–9 plead with God to remember against Edom, and they speak (rhetorically) against Babylon. That means then that the prayer to God in these verses is offered instead of acts of violence. It places the request for justice in the hands of God where it belongs.

• Discuss:

*It is natural to be angry when one is the victim of injustice or when someone takes away something precious. What do you do with your anger?*

*Do you agree with Dr. Creach that God would never promote harm to children? Why? On what do you base your view?*

*When you see news reports of children being injured and killed in the crossfire of regional conflicts, what prayer do you offer? Is it an angry prayer? Why?*

*How do you relate the anger Psalm 137 expresses to the New Testament injunction "Be angry but do not sin; do not let the sun go down on your anger, and do not make room for the devil" (Ephesians 4:26–27)?*

- Review "The Church: Offering Prayers for Justice" (pp. 37–38). Share these key points:
  a. Recognizing the justice orientation of the Lord's Prayer helps us see more clearly that Jesus regularly acted to combat the evil he saw. Jesus is gentle, meek, and mild when dealing with people who are weak and vulnerable, but he shows strength against the oppressive forces at work against such people.
  b. The people of God rightly take part in Jesus' action against evil; prayer is a primary means for doing so.
  c. Psalm 137 suggests two steps to praying against injustice: Acknowledge injustice in prayer, and pray for God to act against injustice.
- Discuss:

*In what ways does your church acknowledge injustice in prayer?*

*How does your congregation pray for God to act against injustice?*

- In 2014 the Nobel Peace prize was awarded to Malala Yousafzai, a seventeen-year-old from Pakistan. She campaigned for the right of women to receive an education after the Taliban began attacking girls' schools. She was wounded by a shooter on her school bus but recovered. She continues to stand up against injustice and has been a model for those who see the differences their voices and actions can make. Show the trailer for the movie *He Named Me Malala*, which is available on YouTube. Discuss:

*How would you like to make a difference with your life, even if it does not lead to a Nobel Prize?*

## Conclusion

Name a group of people who currently suffer injustice because of their racial, political, or religious identity or some other identifying characteristic. Then write a prayer for God to bring justice and equity to them. Include in your prayer a description of the wrongs they suffer and a petition for God to act for them.

## Passing the Peace

The peace of Christ be with you.

And also with you.

**Amen.**

# Glossary*

**covenant.** The binding or establishing of a bond between two parties.

**exile.** The period of the Jews' captivity in ancient Babylon (587–538 BCE). Also known as the Babylonian captivity.

**hallelujah.** A transliteration of the two Hebrew words that mean "praise the Lord."

**lament.** A petition for help in affliction. A prayer about things gone wrong—a "prayer request" psalm.

**metaphor.** A comparison in which one thing is said to be another thing ("the LORD *is* my shepherd" in Psalm 23:1).

**parallelism.** Most line segments in Hebrew poetry use parallelism: They say something similar in multiple ways, giving us several ways to grasp the poet's meaning.

**psalm.** The Hebrew name given to hymns or songs of praise.

**Psalter.** Another name for the book of Psalms.

**royal psalm.** A psalm about the monarchy descended from David. Psalm 2 is a royal psalm that was probably sung at coronations.

**simile.** A comparison between two different things that uses the word *like* or the word *as* to describe a similarity (for example, "He is like a tree").

**torah psalm.** A type of wisdom psalm that extols God's instructions to us. (*Torah* means "law" or "instructions.") Psalm 1 is a torah psalm.

---

\* The definitions here relate to ways these terms are used in this study. Further explorations can be made in other resources, such as Donald K. McKim, *The Westminster Dictionary of Theological Terms*, 2nd ed. (Louisville, KY: Westminster John Knox Press, 2014).

# Want to Know More?

Bonhoeffer, Dietrich. *Psalms: The Prayer Book of the Bible.* Minneapolis: Augsburg Fortress Press, 1974.

Brueggemann, Walter. *The Message of the Psalms: A Theological Commentary.* Minneapolis: Augsburg, 1984.

Creach, Jerome F. D. *The Destiny of the Righteous in the Psalms.* St. Louis: Chalice Press, 2008.

_____. *Psalms.* Interpretation Bible Studies. Louisville, KY: Westminster John Knox Press, 1998.

McCann, J. Clinton, Jr. "The Book of Psalms." In *The New Interpreter's Bible.* Volume 4. Edited by Leander Keck. Nashville: Abingdon Press, 1996.

Mays, James Luther. *The Psalms.* Interpretation: A Bible Commentary for Teaching and Preaching. Louisville, KY: Westminster John Knox Press, 1994.

Printed in the USA
CPSIA information can be obtained
at www.ICGtesting.com
CBHW070950010424
6173CB00008B/65